Tons of Money

A Farce in Three Acts

Will Evans and Arthur Valentine

A SAMUEL FRENCH ACTING EDITION

SAMUELFRENCH-LONDON.CO.UK
SAMUELFRENCH.COM

Copyright © 1927 by Samuel French Ltd
Copyright © in renewal 1955 by Archibald Thomas Pechey
All Rights Reserved

TONS OF MONEY is fully protected under the copyright laws of the British Commonwealth, including Canada, the United States of America, and all other countries of the Copyright Union. All rights, including professional and amateur stage productions, recitation, lecturing, public reading, motion picture, radio broadcasting, television and the rights of translation into foreign languages are strictly reserved.

ISBN 978-0-573-01450-5

www.samuelfrench-london.co.uk

www.samuelfrench.com

For Amateur Production Enquiries

United Kingdom and World excluding North America

plays@SamuelFrench-London.co.uk

020 7255 4302/01

Each title is subject to availability from Samuel French,

depending upon country of performance.

CAUTION: Professional and amateur producers are hereby warned that *TONS OF MONEY* is subject to a licensing fee. Publication of this play does not imply availability for performance. Both amateurs and professionals considering a production are strongly advised to apply to the appropriate agent before starting rehearsals, advertising, or booking a theatre. A licensing fee must be paid whether the title is presented for charity or gain and whether or not admission is charged.

The professional rights in this play are controlled by Samuel French Ltd, 52 Fitzroy Street, London, W1T 5JR.

No one shall make any changes in this title for the purpose of production. No part of this book may be reproduced, stored in a retrieval system, or transmitted in any form, by any means, now known or yet to be invented, including mechanical, electronic, photocopying, recording, videotaping, or otherwise, without the prior written permission of the publisher. No one shall upload this title, or part of this title, to any social media websites.

The right of Will Evans and Arthur Valentine to be identified as author of this work has been asserted by them in accordance with Section 77 of the Copyright, Designs and Patents Act 1988

TONS OF MONEY

Produced at the Opera House, Southport, on March 20th, 1922. Transferred to the Shaftesbury Theatre, London, on April 13th, 1922, and to the Aldwych Theatre, London, on October 30th, 1922. The play was withdrawn on January 29th, 1924, after a run of 733 performances.

CHARACTERS
(In Order of Appearance)

SPRULES (a Butler)	Mr. George Barrett.
SIMPSON (a Parlourmaid)	Miss Ena Mason.
MISS BENITA MULLETT	Miss Mary Brough.
LOUISE ALLINGTON	Miss Yvonne Arnaud.
AUBREY HENRY MAITLAND ALLINGTON	Mr. Ralph Lynn.
GILES (a Gardener)	Mr. Willie Warde.
JAMES CHESTERMAN (a Solicitor)	Mr. J. Robertson Hare
JEAN EVERARD	Miss Madge Saunders.
HENERY	Mr. Tom Walls.
GEORGE MAITLAND	Mr. Sydney Lynn.

SCENES

ACT I
SCENE.—*Aubrey Henry Maitland Allington's house at Marlow.*
(*Three weeks elapse between Acts I and II.*)

ACT II
SCENE.—*The same.* (*Afternoon.*)
(*One day elapses between Acts II and III.*)

ACT III
SCENE.—*The same.* (*Late afternoon.*)

TONS OF MONEY

ACT I

SCENE.—*Library of* AUBREY HENRY MAITLAND ALLINGTON'S *house at Marlow. The room is handsomely furnished.*

At back C.—*somewhat deeply recessed—double French windows, approached from the room by shallow steps, open to a terrace, and command a view of the river and the landscape beyond. In the recess and to the* L. *of the window, built into the wall, is a bookcase, and below this, in the angle of the room facing the audience, a door.*

At the extreme L. *of the room is a low-backed arm-chair, and behind it, against the wall, a bronze statuette with an electrolier. Below the window* L.C. *a large settle couch with cushions is set at an angle facing* R., *and immediately above it, and at its* R. *end, a small, square table on which is a telephone.*

In the R. *wall of the window recess, facing the bookcase, is a low cabinet, and in the wall above it a speaking-tube. On the* R. *of this, in the wall facing the audience, stands a grandfather's clock.*

On the R. *of the clock,* R.C. *in the back flat, are large double doors which lead to a passage from which a stairway rises to the* R., *and at the foot of the stairway a large leaded window.*

The square, stone fireplace is in the R. *wall, with bronze and irons in the hearth and a fender stool against the high curb. Above it a small dinner waggon.*

R.C. *is a gate-legged table, which at the rise of the curtain is laid for breakfast: there is a small chair above it and one is set on its* R.

A winged arm-chair immediately below the fireplace and a smaller one facing it.

The room has a high panelling, and the plain walls above this are decorated with tapestries.

TIME.—*Morning.*

(*As the* CURTAIN *rises the telephone bell rings; after a slight pause it rings again—enter* SPRULES *through double doors; he is dressed in butler's morning clothes, is severe and precise in his manner, is slightly grey and wears side-whiskers. He carries a silver salver which he puts down as he takes up the telephone.*)

SPRULES. Hello! Hello! Yes, this is Mr. Allington's house. No, sir, the master isn't down yet. I expect him any hour now, sir. What name please, sir? Ches—Chester—Mr. Chesterman. Very good, sir. I'll tell him you rang up. (*Replaces receiver and goes to breakfast table, picks up letters, writs, etc.*)

(*Enter* SIMPSON *through double doors carrying tray with hot dishes, coffee and milk, which she places on sideboard, up stage* R. *She is a smart parlourmaid.*)

SIMPSON. Anything excitin', Mr. Sprules ?
SPRULES. Nothing much ! (*Taking up letters.*) Hello, here we are again. Bill ! Bill ! Bill ! (*Smells one.*) Lady ! (*Glances over other letters.*) And more bills !
SIMPSON. Who's got most ? (*Puts hot plates on breakfast table.*)
SPRULES. About fifty-fifty.
SIMPSON. I never saw such a 'ouse. ⎱ (*During this, business*
SPRULES. And you never will again. ⎰ *of arranging breakfast*
SIMPSON. Do they ever pay anybody ? ⎱ *table.*)
SPRULES (L.). Not if they can help it. ⎰
SIMPSON (R.). I wonder the blooming creditors waste paper and ink sending the bills in. (*Placing hot coffee and milk on table.*)
SPRULES. Creditors, Miss Simpson, are like fishermen and lovers, they exist on hopes.

(*Enter* MISS BENITA MULLETT *from the garden. She is an elderly lady dressed in black or mauve, white hair and spectacles. She is very prim in manner, but always speaks abruptly, very deaf and rather fussy. She comes down* L.)

MISS MULLETT. Simpson, have you seen my knitting ?
SIMPSON. No, ma'am. (*Placing toast rack on table.*)
MISS MULLETT. One can't keep anything in this house. (*Crosses in front of table* R.C. *to* R., *sees breakfast table.*) What ! Breakfast not over yet !
SIMPSON. Master and mistress just coming down, ma'am.
MISS MULLETT. What !
SPRULES (*loudly*). Master and mistress are just coming down, ma'am. (*Places chair for* AUBREY *at back of table which is set for two.*)
MISS MULLETT. All right, don't shout, I'm not deaf. (*Takes morning paper from back of chair set at* R. *of table for* LOUISE.)

(*Exit* SIMPSON *through double doors.*)

I never saw such a house ! When I was a girl we always had breakfast at eight o'clock. (*Sits in chair down* R. *near fireplace.*)

(*Enter* MRS. LOUISE ALLINGTON *from staircase. She is a young and pretty woman of about four-and-twenty, very smartly dressed.*)

LOUISE. Good morning, Auntie Ben ! (*Round* L. *of table to* MISS MULLETT).
MISS MULLETT (*severely*). Good afternoon, my dear. (*Gives her cheek to be kissed.*)

(LOUISE *kisses her cheek.*)

D'you know it's eleven o'clock.

LOUISE. Well, dear, what of it ? (*Sits down R. of table and begins to look at her letters.*)

(SPRULES, *who has remained at top of table, takes the covers off dishes and exits through double doors.*)

MISS MULLETT. Where's your husband ?

LOUISE (*reading letter*). Aubrey will be down soon—he's in his bath.

MISS MULLETT. The hours you and Aubrey keep, my dear, are a perfect disgrace.

LOUISE. I loathe early rising.

MISS MULLETT. The early bird catches the worm, my dear.

LOUISE. Well, if there's only one worm, auntie, why should I spoil the market. (*Pouring out coffee.*)

MISS MULLETT. Your husband is worse than you are !

LOUISE. Aubrey has the artistic temperament.

MISS MULLETT. What's that ?

(*Enter* AUBREY HENRY MAITLAND ALLINGTON *down staircase and through double doors. He is a tall clean-shaven man of about thirty-five. He wears a smart lounge suit and monocle, and has a careless off-hand manner. He goes up to window, stands with his back to the audience, business of inhaling the air and doing dumbbell exercises. He then comes down stage.*)

AUBREY. That's wonderful ! Those bath salts have gone straight to my head. (*Comes down and goes to* LOUISE.) Good morning, all. (*At his place at table, taking cover off entrée dish.*) Good morning, fish ; good afternoon, rolls. (*Picking up bills.*) Good night, bills. (*Noticing* MISS MULLETT.) Good morning, Auntie Ben . . . (*Goes R. He places his finger on her cheek and makes a kissing noise with his lips.*) Brighter London ! The warmth of her welcome quite unnerves me. (*Sits at breakfast table centre back.*)

LOUISE (*reading*). Here's a letter from Cousin Jean, Aubrey. She's coming for the week-end.

AUBREY. I've got bad news too. (*Flourishing letters.*)

MISS MULLETT. I was just asking what the artistic temperament was, Aubrey.

AUBREY. The artistic temperament, Auntie Ben, is a disinclination to work, and an aversion to soap and water.

LOUISE. I'm sorry, dear. I just said you had it.

AUBREY. Oh, darling, don't say that ! I wear my hair short, and have two baths a day. (*Serves fish to* LOUISE *and himself.*)

LOUISE (*reading letter*). You know, Aubrey, I'm fed up with this woman.

AUBREY. Cousin Jean

LOUISE. No, this dressmaker of mine.
AUBREY. Wants money?
LOUISE. Yes.
AUBREY. I'll send her a cheque.
LOUISE. Don't be silly, dear, it wouldn't be met.
AUBREY. I beg your pardon, the day the bank refuses to meet my cheques, I shall take my overdraft elsewhere.
MISS MULLETT (*reading newspaper, not heeding their conversation*). An extensive V-shaped depression is rapidly approaching from the North Sea.
AUBREY. That's Cousin Jean.
MISS MULLETT (*still reading*). Stormy weather may be expected. Louise, you had better see about my goloshes.

(*During this* AUBREY *takes writ out of envelope.*)

LOUISE. Yes, auntie, I will. (*To* AUBREY.) What's that funny paper you've got there?
AUBREY. That's a writ.
LOUISE. Really, what for?
AUBREY. For those cigars you gave me on my last birthday.
LOUISE. It's a pity you smoke so much, Aubrey.
AUBREY. Smoke! I gave those cigars to the gardener. He's cleared the garden of blight. (*Reading from another letter.*) Now what the dickens does this mean?
LOUISE. Does what mean?

(*Enter* SPRULES *from doors* R., *comes down* L. *of table.*)

SPRULES. Oh, I forgot to tell you, sir, a Mr. Chesterman rang up this morning.
AUBREY (*reading*). Any message?
SPRULES. He asked if you were down, sir, and I said you weren't up.
AUBREY (*laughing*). You mean he asked if I was up, and you said I wasn't down. That's very good! (*Attempts to shake hands, then realizes that it is* SPRULES *he is talking to.*)
SPRULES. Er—yes, sir.
AUBREY. All right, Sprules.
SPRULES. Very good, sir.

(*Exit* SPRULES R. *through double doors.*)

AUBREY. He must be the fellow who's written this letter. (*Reading.*) Chesterman, Chesterman & Chesterman, Lincoln's Inn Fields.
LOUISE. Why do West End solicitors always have three names in the firms?
AUBREY. All the most dangerous things go in threes. Three Star brandy. Three-card trick. Three brass balls.

LOUISE. What does it say ?
AUBREY (*reading*). "Dear Sir——" (*To* LOUISE, *aside*.) He calls me dear. "Our Mr. James Chesterman will call on you to-morrow morning at eleven o'clock to acquaint you with a matter of considerable importance to yourself. Faithfully yours, Chesterman, Chesterman (*turning over letter*) & Chesterman." (*Thoughtfully*.) Now is that a threat or a promise ?
LOUISE. He's either got some money to give us, or else wants some of ours.
AUBREY. Darling, he's a solicitor.
MISS MULLETT. Who's a solicitor ?
LOUISE. Mr. Chesterman, auntie.
MISS MULLETT. Who's Mr. Chesterman ?
AUBREY (*standing*). The fellow we're talking about.
MISS MULLETT. Why ?
AUBREY (*loudly and impatiently*). He's coming here.
MISS MULLETT. Don't shout, I'm not deaf. When's he coming ?
AUBREY. Any moment.
MISS MULLETT. What ?
AUBREY. Any moment !
MISS MULLETT. Then I'm going. (*Turns up towards double doors.*)
My father used to say lawyers were like leeches,

(AUBREY *rises and goes to open doors for her.*)

only leeches do let you go sometimes.

(*Exit* MISS MULLETT *through double doors.*)

AUBREY (*resuming breakfast*). I love having Auntie Ben here, she worries me to death. (*Sitting down.*)
LOUISE. Poor dear Auntie, she means well.
AUBREY (*reading letter*). Does she; then, of course, there's no hope for her.
LOUISE. By the way, dear, Jannaway——
AUBREY. January ?
LOUISE. No, Jannaway !—called yesterday to see you. He wondered if you've forgotten you owe him a £100.
AUBREY. Tell him I have quite forgotten it.
LOUISE. I've a letter here from Robinson too—
AUBREY. Robinson Crusoe ?
LOUISE (*holding letter*). —saying that if his account isn't paid next week, he'll commence proceedings.
AUBREY. Well, I'm not stopping him.
LOUISE. No; but, Aubrey, do be serious. One can't run bills for ever.
AUBREY. One can try.
LOUISE. What about your new invention ?

AUBREY. Which one, the hair restorer, the blasting powder, or the rat remover?

LOUISE. The blasting powder.

AUBREY. Oh! Gadinite? That's going to make our fortune

LOUISE. Fortune! How?

AUBREY. Why, it's the most wonderful explosive that's ever been dreamt of. Now say you're making a railway.

LOUISE. I'm making a railway.

AUBREY. No, darling, I don't want you to say it. I mean imagine you're making a railway, you come to a mountain, what do you do?

LOUISE. Look at it.

AUBREY. No, blast it . . . when you've done that the mountain's gone.

LOUISE. Where's it gone to?

AUBREY. Blown sky-high! D'you realize (*impressively*) that one pinch of this powder, just as much as you could put on a . . . sixpence, is enough to blow up the whole of half London—er—er—the half of whole London.

LOUISE (*awestruck*). Aubrey, are you going to sell your blasted powder in sixpenny packets?

AUBREY (*laughing*). It's going to make our fortune, that's all.

LOUISE. Why, it'll be worth . . . what will it be worth, Aubrey?

AUBREY. One million and four pounds.

LOUISE. Aubrey, but surely you can't be certain of the four.

AUBREY. It's the four I am certain of.

LOUISE (*after a pause*). Then why not give a dinner-party to all the people we owe money to? . . .

AUBREY. We'd have to take the Albert Hall.

LOUISE. And tell them about your new invention. It might keep them quiet.

AUBREY. You don't seem to realize that the people we've got to invite are the people we've got to go to to supply the dinner.

LOUISE. But that's my point. We invite them to dinner and order the materials for the dinner from them. If they refuse our orders they won't get any dinner, and if they accept them they will be sure to come.

AUBREY. Knowing they never get paid in any case.

(GILES *appears at French windows. He is a typical old gardener, wearing flannel shirt, corduroy trousers, green baize apron and heavy boots. He is carrying his hat, in which are three eggs.*)

LOUISE. I think it's a fine idea. I think I'm going to write something like this: "Dear Mr. Brown, Will you and your wife come and dine with us on Thursday. P.S. Kindly send me up a case of champagne." They can't refuse.

(GILES *comes down stage.*)

AUBREY. I shan't know what to talk to them about.

LOUISE. It doesn't matter, we owe them all money. They'll have lots in common; besides, think how Jean will enjoy it.

AUBREY. Yes, I don't suppose she knows a third of the people we owe money to.

(*By this time* GILES *has reached the settle and very slowly takes the eggs one by one and places them on a cushion on settle.*)

LOUISE. Well, Giles?

GILES (*taking his time to answer*). Eggs! (*Ambles slowly up stage.*)

(*Exit through French windows.*)

(AUBREY *and* LOUISE *both watching him intently until he disappears.*)

AUBREY. Little chatterbox! Why does he lay the eggs in here —er—bring the eggs in here?

LOUISE. Poor old soul, he's proposed to cook and she's refused him, so he won't go near the kitchen. (*Looking round the room.*) Of course it's the expense of this big place that's doing all the mischief.

AUBREY. Don't be silly, darling, there's only one way to get credit, that is make people believe you've got miles more money than you have.

LOUISE. They can easily do that with us; look at this room for instance, anyone coming in here . . .

AUBREY. Well, what's wrong with this? (*Taking up letter.*) That coat-of-arms isn't right, I admit, (*indicating one over fireplace*) it ought to be a couple of bailiffs rampant. (*Reading letter.*) Oh, Lord, that's done it . . .

LOUISE. Done what?

AUBREY. That account of Mannerings, they got judgment against us, you know; this letter says that unless £500 is paid within a week I'm bankrupt. Don't worry, darling, that's a bit of fun.

LOUISE. It's not much use giving that dinner then.

(*Enter* SPRULES *through double doors, stands* R. *of doorway.*)

SPRULES. Mr. Chesterman, sir.

AUBREY (*rising*). More trouble.

(*Enter* JAMES CHESTERMAN *through double doors. He is a clean-shaven man, very precise in manner, neatly dressed, gold pince-nez, carries attaché-case, hands his silk hat to* SPRULES *on entering.*)

(*Exit* SPRULES *through double doors.*)

CHESTERMAN (*crossing down left behind* AUBREY, *who is seated at table*). Mr. Allington?

(AUBREY *bus., of turning* R., *misses* CHESTERMAN *on entering. On hearing his voice turns* L., *and sees him standing* L.)

AUBREY. Ah, there you are, Mr. Chesterman. (*Shakes hands.*)

LOUISE (*rising*). I'd better go, Aubrey.

AUBREY. No, no, no. Stay, dear. Mr. Chesterman, my wife, my fish. (*Takes attaché-case from* CHESTERMAN, *walks round looking for somewhere to place it, finally hands it back to* CHESTERMAN.) Will you have some breakfast?

CHESTERMAN. No, thank you, I always breakfast at eight.

AUBREY. We always dine at eight. Please sit down. (*Indicating settle.*) Oh, excuse me. (*Takes eggs from cushion and places them in ash tray on table* L.C.) The gardener laid these—er—er—put them there.

CHESTERMAN (*sitting on settle*). I wrote you last night, Mr. Allington. My name is Chesterman, of the firm of Chesterman, Chesterman & Chesterman of Lincoln's Inn Fields.

AUBREY (*sits at breakfast table*). Yes. I've just this moment opened your letter.

CHESTERMAN. You'll permit me to ask you a few questions?

AUBREY. Certainly, certainly and certainly.

CHESTERMAN. I'm right, I think, in believing that you are Aubrey Henry Maitland Allington?

AUBREY. Yes, all of them. (*Brings his chair to* R.C., *puts serviette and plate on his knee, going on with his breakfast.*)

CHESTERMAN. Son of the late Charles Maitland Allington of Wintercroft in the county of Devon.

AUBREY. I've always understood so.

CHESTERMAN. You have a brother, John Whittingham Allington.

AUBREY (*tersely*). Yes, but that's not my fault.

CHESTERMAN. Please answer my question, Mr. Allington. Is that so?

AUBREY. I regret to say it is.

CHESTERMAN. That is an expression I can neither endorse nor contradict.

AUBREY. You never knew my brother.

CHESTERMAN. I didn't.

AUBREY. Obviously.

CHESTERMAN. Mr. Allington, your brother I believe once did you some injury.

AUBREY. You're right. (*Putting plate back on table and rising.*) It was *some* injury. He married the only girl I ever loved!

LOUISE. Aubrey! (*Springing up.*)

AUBREY. Oh, before I met you. (*Takes up entrée-dish and polishes it unconsciously.*)

LOUISE. Yes, but you never told me.

AUBREY. I was too broke—broken-hearted. My brother's last action—Mr. Chesterman, my brother's last action——

CHESTERMAN. Mr. Allington, your brother's last action was to—die a week ago. (*Standing down, a little* L.)
AUBREY (*crossing* R. *to fireplace*). I'm sorry!
CHESTERMAN. Your brother has left you——
AUBREY (*scornfully*). His kind wishes?
CHESTERMAN. A life interest in his entire fortune.

(*Business of trying to put his hand in his pocket.*)

LOUISE (*standing by her chair, in surprise*). A life interest in his entire fortune?
CHESTERMAN. Yes, madam—expressing at the same time his sincere regrets for any injury he might have done you.

(*There is a pause.*)

LOUISE (*thoughtfully*). I wonder if it's too late to send the dear fellow a nice wreath?
AUBREY (*to* LOUISE). Allow me, dear, the head of the house. Mr. Chesterman, what can I say? (*Crosses* L.C. *in front of table.*)
LOUISE (*reprovingly*). Nothing, dear.
AUBREY. Nothing, dear.
CHESTERMAN. The estate—I am quoting from figures sent me from Mexico—amounts roughly to four hundred and seventy thousand dollars. (*Sits* C. *of settle.*)
AUBREY (*excitedly walking up and down stage* C.) Four—hundred and seventy thousand—dollars!!!
CHESTERMAN. Yes.

(AUBREY *gazes at him for a moment and then begins to laugh,* LOUISE *joining in.*)

AUBREY (*cross* L.). I'll buy it.
CHESTERMAN (*puzzled*). You'll buy what, Mr. Allington?
AUBREY. Yes—I mean, what am I expected to say? (*About to rest his foot on settle—does so on telephone table—realizes his mistake—then puts it down.*)
CHESTERMAN. I'm afraid I don't understand you.
AUBREY. Well, what's the joke?
CHESTERMAN. Mr. Allington, I don't know what you're driving at. If you are casting aspersions on my—— (*Rises.*)
AUBREY (*seeing* CHESTERMAN *is getting rattled, smoothes his head*). No, no, no! I beg your pardon! But is it really true?
CHESTERMAN. Here is the will. (*Takes will from pocket.*)

(AUBREY *takes will from* CHESTERMAN; LOUISE *in turn, advancing to* R.C., *takes it from* AUBREY.)

AUBREY. And it amounts to what, you say?
CHESTERMAN. As far as can be at present ascertained, four hundred and seventy thousand dollars.

LOUISE. I think he might have left it in pounds. (*Studying will, below table* R.C.)

CHESTERMAN. In Mexico they speak of everything in dollars, madam. (*Goes* L.)

LOUISE. Are there sixteen dollars to the pound, Aubrey, same as ounces?

AUBREY. It depends on the height of the sea-level, darling.

CHESTERMAN. Your interest, Mr. Allington, is only a life one.

AUBREY. That won't worry me. (*Goes up stage.*)

(LOUISE *sits* R. *of table, listening.*)

CHESTERMAN. In the event of your death, the money passes to your cousin, George Maitland of Mexico.

AUBREY. He'll never get it. (*Coming down* C.)

CHESTERMAN. And why not, pray?

AUBREY. He's gone to a place where they don't issue return tickets.

CHESTERMAN. I beg your pardon.

AUBREY. Cousin George had a sticky end in a whisky saloon in Mexico.

CHESTERMAN. So I've heard, Mr. Allington, but no one seems to know positively what actually occurred.

AUBREY. The only other party who could tell us, Mr. Chesterman, was so full of George's bullets that he had no further interest in the proceedings.

CHESTERMAN. All the same we have no actual proof of death.

AUBREY. No, George had the proof.

CHESTERMAN. All the same, we are advertising for him.

AUBREY. Well, unless they issue asbestos editions I don't think it will reach him.

CHESTERMAN. Still, Mr. Allington, dead or alive, let's hope he won't be wanted for a long time.

AUBREY. I entirely agree.

CHESTERMAN. And now I must leave you, merely congratulating you on your good fortune, and hoping you will both live long to enjoy it. (LOUISE *rises, going up* R.)

(*During this* AUBREY *takes* CHESTERMAN'S *hand, notes he is wearing a ring, and examines it closely.*)

AUBREY (*shaking hands*). Spoken like a true friend and a Special Constable. (*Unconsciously taking up an egg from the table, and offering it to* CHESTERMAN.) Have an egg? Oh, I beg your pardon. (*Sits* L.)

CHESTERMAN (*crossing to* LOUISE, *who is standing up stage* R.). Good-bye, Mrs. Allington. (*Shakes hands.*) I will leave you that copy of the will. (*Indicating will on breakfast table.*) If there is any immediate advance——

AUBREY. What's that?

LOUISE. Immediate advance, dear.

AUBREY (*excitedly—crossing to* CHESTERMAN *as he goes towards double doors*). Oh, yes, yes, certainly, make it as immediate as possible. Good-bye, Mr. Chesterman, good-bye. It can't be too immediate.

(*Exit* CHESTERMAN *through double doors.*)

(AUBREY *standing at double doors, shouts after him.*)

Good-bye, Mr. Chesterman! Take any hat you like!

(LOUISE *comes down* R., AUBREY *comes down* C., *both showing great excitement. They stand facing one another.*)

LOUISE. Aubrey, I think I want to scream or dance!

AUBREY. Well, darling, scream and dance, we can afford it, now!

(*Both rush to one another, embrace, laughing loudly and excitedly.*)

(*Enter* SPRULES *hurriedly through double doors; he stands* R.C., *amazed, as they both stop guiltily.* AUBREY *is looking over* LOUISE'S *shoulder.*)

SPRULES (R.). Did you call, sir?

AUBREY (L.C.). No, n-no, Sprules, we were merely screaming, that's all.

SPRULES. Very good, sir.

(SPRULES, *looking puzzled, exits and closes the door.*)

(LOUISE *and* AUBREY *resume their former excitement,* AUBREY *throws cushions about, takes pile of letters, bills, etc., from table.*)

AUBREY. Look, darling. (*Throws bills in the air.*) There they go, full pack. (*Falls into his chair at table* R.C.) I feel better now.

LOUISE (*falling into arm-chair* R.). So do I.

AUBREY. Now where's that will? (*Not seeing it at first, is perturbed.*) Darling, it was here a minute ago. I haven't thrown it away, have I?

LOUISE (*helping him to find it, picks up writ from table.*) Here it is, darling.

AUBREY (*taking it from her, and throwing it back on the table*). No, that's a summons, dear. Ah, there's the will. (*Taking it from table.*) Now, let's have a look at it. (*He becomes very important, pulls his chair to* L. *of table.*) Don't get excited, darling; have you never had money left you before? I have, all mine's left me. (*Reading from will—places his foot on chair* L. *of table.*) I, John Whittingham Allington, being of sound mind . . .

LOUISE. What, dear? *(Coming behind table and looking over his shoulder.)*

AUBREY. Being of sound mind, dear. They have to put that in to account for his going to a solicitor.

LOUISE. I see.

AUBREY. I give, bequeath and devise all my real and personal estate of which I may die possessed or to whom I may hereinafter become entitled together with all lands, estates, here—here—dit . . .

LOUISE. Here-dit-a-ments.

AUBREY. Here-dit-a-ments, tenements, massages . .

LOUISE. Mes*suages*.

AUBREY. Sewages or any other properties.

LOUISE. I see now why they put that bit in about the sound mind.

AUBREY. Never mind, we don't want to understand it. We'll take a month's holiday and study it. *(Folds it up and places it in drawer of table by settle* L.C.*)* Four hundred and seventy thousand dollars. *(Turning and taking* LOUISE'S *hands.)*

LOUISE. Four hundred and seventy thousand dollars.

AUBREY. That's about one hundred and twenty thousand pounds, about six thousand a year. Why, it's a fortune! *(Picks up receiver of telephone.)* Am I there? Yes. *(Replaces receiver.)*

LOUISE. There's simply nothing we can't afford. *(Sitting armchair* R.*)*

AUBREY. One hundred and twenty thousand pounds! We can pay off every bill we owe. *(Goes to settle.)*

LOUISE. What's that?

AUBREY. I say we can pay off every bill we owe. *(Sitting on settle.)*

LOUISE. Yes, but——

AUBREY. But what, we've got tons of money. *(On settle.)*

LOUISE *(deliberately)*. But we owe tons of money, Aubrey, and by the time we've paid for the tons of money, there won't be any tons of money left. *(Rises and stands by breakfast table.)*

AUBREY. And we'll be bankrupt next week. *(Rises. Gets* C.*)*

LOUISE. It will all be taken by the official retriever.

AUBREY. Oh, Lord, I'd forgotten that.

LOUISE. But our creditors won't. *(Sits chair* R. *of table* R.C.*)*

AUBREY. They'll simply swarm round us now. *(Sits on chair he has moved to* L. *of table.)*

LOUISE. Of course they will.

AUBREY. Like a flock of wasps.

LOUISE. Do wasps flock, Aubrey?

AUBREY. Yes, if they want to.

LOUISE. Oh, I never knew they did.

AUBREY. Whom do we owe money to?

LOUISE. Every one we've ever dealt with.

AUBREY. Shall I make a list? *(Picking up an envelope from table* R.C., *crosses* L.*)*

LOUISE. Of the people we owe money to?
AUBREY (*turning to her*). No, of the people we don't—it would be miles quicker.
LOUISE. Aubrey, don't fool. (*Goes up stage* R.C.) It's too serious.
AUBREY. It's perfectly disgusting, you know, the way people give credit. (*Sits on settle.*)
LOUISE (*walks round up to French windows*). I think they ought to make it a criminal offence.
AUBREY. They simply don't deserve to be paid!
LOUISE. Besides, think how hurt your brother would be if he thought we'd used his money to give to people he didn't even know. (*Coming down* C.)
AUBREY. Well, what are we to do?
LOUISE. Is it necessary for our creditors to know we've come into money? (*Crosses* R.)
AUBREY. My dear girl, how can we prevent it? They're bound to know.
LOUISE. Yes, I suppose so.
AUBREY. Of course they'd know if I had five shillings. They'd know like a shot.

(*Pause.*)

LOUISE (*suddenly*). Aubrey, I've got an idea!
AUBREY. What?
LOUISE. What happens if you die?
AUBREY. I shall probably be buried.
LOUISE. Don't be absurd! I mean, who gets the money?
AUBREY. George Maitland, my first cousin. Chesterman just told us so!
LOUISE. But you say he's dead.
AUBREY. So he is.
LOUISE. Sure?
AUBREY. Absolutely. Positive!
LOUISE. Then why not—bring him—to life again. (*One knee on chair* R.C., *as she faces* AUBREY, *who is still seated on settle.*)
AUBREY. D'you think I'm a corpse reviver?
LOUISE. You're very dense, dear! If once we can kill *you*——
AUBREY. Eh?
LOUISE. If once we can make people believe you're dead, you can come to life again as George Maitland, your cousin, and claim all the money.

(AUBREY *contemplates her slowly as her meaning dawns on him.*)

AUBREY. By Jove, what a brain wave. (*Rises, crosses to* LOUISE.)
LOUISE. That's what I thought.
AUBREY. You mean——? Let's figure this out!

(AUBREY *takes* LOUISE *to settle, they sit down close to each other.* AUBREY *down stage.*)

LOUISE. You've got to die! And there must be no mistake about it.

AUBREY. But how am I going to die?

LOUISE. Never mind that now. You're dead!

AUBREY. Yes.

LOUISE. Your will is read. You leave everything to me!

AUBREY. But, darling, there's nothing to leave.

LOUISE. Exactly, that's what I'm driving at!

AUBREY. What's the good if there's—— Oh, I see! And so the poor dog had none. (*Points to bills on table.*) The Retriever!

LOUISE. Quite so. Exit crowd of sorrowing creditors.

(AUBREY *goes* C. *Both burst out laughing.* LOUISE *remains seated on settle.*)

AUBREY. Can't you see them all coming to the funeral with eyes full of writs and pockets full of tears? (*Imitating a Jewish moneylender's walk.*) Well, I'm dead—now what happens? (*Sits again, close to* LOUISE.)

LOUISE. Now George Maitland appears.

AUBREY. I see—that's me.

LOUISE. Exactly—what's George like?

(AUBREY *crosses to sideboard* R., *and brings family album out of drawer, comes down* C.)

AUBREY. I've got a photograph of the whole family—dating from 1784—with finger-prints. There you are—that's George as he was before he went to Mexico. (*Business of turning pages over and over.*)

(LOUISE *rises and comes* C., *looks very closely at photographs—pages touch the end of her nose.*)

And here's the photo he sent after he'd been out there a few years.

LOUISE. Oh, is that George? How tall is he?

AUBREY. Oh, he's a fine-looking, big strapping chap—just about my build. (*Bracing himself up as he says this.*)

LOUISE. Could you make yourself look like that, Aubrey?

AUBREY. Oh, easily.

LOUISE. But he's quite good looking.

AUBREY. Exactly.

LOUISE. Then that's settled. (*Puts album on settle.*) Chesterman has advertised for you, I mean for George. (*She sits on settle.*)

AUBREY. Yes, don't you remember he said so? (*Sits on settle.*)

(*Both on settle,* AUBREY *up stage end of settle.*)

LOUISE. Well then, after you're dead, wait a few weeks, and then send a wire to Chesterman: "Just landed in England. Seen your advertisement. I am on my way down. George Maitland."

AUBREY. Shall I be able to stay here?

LOUISE. Of course! We're cousins!

AUBREY. And after everything's fixed up, we can get married.

LOUISE. How ripping! (*Sits closer to* AUBREY—*affectionately.*) Fancy having a second honeymoon with one's own husband.

AUBREY. It's never done, darling, but we'll try it. Now, the next thing is——

(*Enter* SPRULES *double doors.* AUBREY *turns round quickly.* SPRULES *comes down to* MISS MULLETT'S *chair* R., *and moves cushions as if looking for something.*)

What do you want, Sprules?

SPRULES. Miss Mullett wants to know if she left her wool here, sir?

AUBREY (*rises and goes* C. *towards* SPRULES). Tell Miss Mullett to go to the dev—to the dining-room—no, don't tell her that! No, it isn't here!

SPRULES. Very good, sir.

(*Exit* SPRULES *through double doors.*)

LOUISE. Well, how are you going to die?

AUBREY. I don't know, I've never done it before. (*Sits on settle.*)

LOUISE. We've got to bury you too.

AUBREY. Well, don't harp on it.

LOUISE. Then after the funeral—— We mustn't forget to put it in all the papers.

AUBREY (*regarding* LOUISE *fixedly*). Have you made a hobby of this sort of thing?

LOUISE. No, dear, but it's most essential that there shouldn't be any doubt whatsoever regarding your death. (*Rises and crosses round back of breakfast table to fireplace* R.)

AUBREY (*grimly*). There won't be any by the time you've finished with me.

LOUISE. Well, we *must* get the details right.

AUBREY. Don't get them too right, remember I'm only an imitation corpse.

LOUISE. No, I won't, dear. (*Coming to* C.) Now, who shall we invite to the funeral? (*Sits* R. *of* AUBREY *on settle.*)

AUBREY (*angrily—jumps up and goes* C.). No one! I won't have anyone at all. (*Paces room from* L. *to* R.)

LOUISE. Aubrey!

AUBREY. You're not going to have a picnic at my expense, so don't think it. (*Pauses down* L.)

Louise. But, dear, the look of the thing.

Aubrey. Who cares about the look of the thing? I shan't be there to see it.

Louise. Oh, no, I was thinking you would be.

Aubrey. Well, don't think those things. (*Crosses to telephone table.*) I'll take jolly good care I'm not. (*Sits on edge of telephone table.*)

Louise. What's worrying me is *how* you're going to die.

Aubrey. Exactly, how?

(*A slight pause, during which both think deeply.*)

Louise. What about a nice fit?

Aubrey. Whose feet—oh, fit! Why don't you say fit. "I" before "E" except after "Z." (*Business of imitating a fit.*) Oh, no, thanks, the moment I start throwing fits, Sprules will come and sit on my head.

Louise (*still on settle*). I thought it was rather a good idea.

Aubrey. I'm sorry to differ from you, dear; I think it's a pretty bad idea. People get over fits.

(Aubrey *rests his foot on chair, table* R.C.)

Louise. I'll take good care you don't.

(Aubrey *looks at* Louise *suspiciously.*)

Aubrey (*deliberately*). Well, anyhow—fits—are—off! (*Goes back to his place on settle.*)

(*Another pause.*)

(Louise *rises, in thought, to behind settle.*)

Louise (*thoughtfully*). You wouldn't like to hang yourself on the banisters, dear?

Aubrey. No, I shouldn't.

Louise. Or throw yourself slightly out of the window?

Aubrey. Certainly not. You can't throw yourself slightly out of a window, you either do it all or none at all. (*Rises from settle and goes to fire* R.)

Louise. I thought you might.

Aubrey. Well, think again. (*Sits in arm-chair* R.)

Louise. Aubrey, if you could only cut your throat. *Comes* C.)

Aubrey. What! (*Jumping up from chair.*)

Louise (*hastily*). Oh, not much, darling, only a teeny little bit.

Aubrey. Oh, I thought you meant cut it right off.

Louise. It would be the making of us, Aubrey!

Aubrey. Well, I won't do it. (*Crosses to* L.)

Louise. I was afraid you wouldn't. (*Going slightly* R. *behind breakfast table.*) But you couldn't turn up as George Maitland until you are dead, so you may as well decide quickly how you are going to die.

(AUBREY *sits on settle.*)

(*Enter* GILES *with flowers from French windows.*)

AUBREY. No! If I'm going to die, what I really want is——
GILES. Flowers. (*Places flowers on settle beside* AUBREY.)

(*Exit* GILES *through French windows.*)

AUBREY (*edging away from the flowers*). I've taken a sudden dislike to flowers. How can I be killed at once? (*Moves and sits chair extreme* L.)

(LOUISE, *who has come round table* R.C., *crosses and stands in front of settle.* SPRULES *opens double doors, speaks from there.*)

SPRULES. Any orders for the butcher? (AUBREY *starts.*)
AUBREY (*turns suddenly—sees* SPRULES). No! run away—we're busy.
LOUISE. I'll see you later, Sprules.

(*Exit* SPRULES, *closes double doors.*)

AUBREY. I never saw such a house. One can't even arrange to die quietly.
LOUISE. If I could hasten your end——
AUBREY. You will do that all right.
LOUISE. Well, think of something. I don't want to stay here all day. (*Turns up* C. *of stage to window.*)

(*Enter* SIMPSON *through double doors.*)

SIMPSON. Please, madam, what time would you like dinner to-night?
LOUISE. Oh, any time—half-past seven.
AUBREY. I shan't want any dinner, Simpson.

(LOUISE *signs to* AUBREY *to be quiet.*)

(SIMPSON *exits through double doors.*)

I shall be dining in heaven.
LOUISE (*coming down stage behind settle*). You were always an optimist, Aubrey. (*Laughs.*) Let's put it off until to-morrow. (*Takes flowers and places them on telephone table.*)
AUBREY. I'll do nothing of the sort. I ought to be dead by now.
LOUISE (*very earnestly.*) All right then, you'll die to-day, if I have to kill you with my own hands.
AUBREY. Nice sympathetic creature.

LOUISE. We must find a way.

AUBREY. Well, darling, I've thought over here, and I've thought over there . . .

LOUISE. We can shoot you. (*Walks* R., *thoughtfully*.)

AUBREY. You can't.

LOUISE. And we might poison you——

AUBREY. You've got a mind like a Newgate Calendar.

LOUISE (R.). We could explode you, though!

AUBREY. What? (*Rises, goes* C.)

LOUISE. That's the idea! The blasted powder. (*They meet* C.)

AUBREY. Explode me!!

LOUISE. Yes, we'll have a nice explosion and you can be blown to bits.

AUBREY. Oh! Let me tell you, madam, we are not going to be exploded. I'm sorry—any other time I can do anything to oblige you—— (*Goes* L. *towards settle.* LOUISE *moves to him and seats him on settle.*)

LOUISE. Listen!

(*Both on settle.*)

I want you to go down into your workshop at the bottom of the garden and make a heap of all the most explosive things you've got on one of the tables.

AUBREY (*sarcastically*). Then sit on it, and light a pipe.

LOUISE. You know that speaking-tube in the workshop—the other end of that? (*Goes up stage, points to speaking-tube on wall* C., *and returns to above telephone table.*)

AUBREY. Yes—well?

LOUISE. Draw the table close up to it and put a lighted candle on it so that it stands *touching the end of the speaking-tube.*

AUBREY. Well?

LOUISE. Round the candle you can pile gunpowder with a train leading to all the new blasting powder.

AUBREY. Yes?

LOUISE (*standing above telephone table*). The moment I blow down the tube it will knock the candle over, fire the gunpowder and the whole place will be blown sky-high. There you are!

AUBREY. Pardon me! There I'm *not*.

LOUISE. Of course you're not, you're miles away by then. (*Sits by* AUBREY *on settle again.*) You've told the servants you're not to be disturbed——

AUBREY. Yes?

LOUISE. But five minutes before the explosion you've locked the door, and got away unnoticed.

AUBREY. Oh, and they still think I'm there.

LOUISE. Exactly. At twelve o'clock—I'll come in and say "Where's the master?"

AUBREY. And they'll say : " He's in his workshop, ma'am, and isn't to be disturbed till twelve o'clock."

LOUISE. That's it. Then at twelve o'clock I'll blow down the tube, there'll be a terrible explosion———!!! And they'll spend the rest of the day hunting for pieces of you——

AUBREY. Ripping! (*Roars with laughter.*)

LOUISE. In the meantime, you will have crept up to the attic, pack a bag with all the things you will require for about three weeks, and take all the loose cash you can find about——

AUBREY. I've done that.

LOUISE. Then you can get away when the coast is clear.

AUBREY (*rises—walks round settle, L. end, speaks from back*). Ripping! When shall I turn up as Cousin George?

LOUISE. Give it three weeks, it will look better.

AUBREY. Yes, but in any case I'll ring up before I arrive. (*Kisses her.*) Ha, ha! I'm glad I thought of that idea!

LOUISE (*kneeling on settle*). Of course. Now I'll ring for Sprules. (*Goes to and rings bell at fireplace.*) Remember I shan't blow down the speaking-tube till twelve o'clock.

AUBREY. Funny to think that when next we meet, I shall be dead. (*Both up* C.)

LOUISE. Darling! It will be the wisest thing you've ever done. Good-bye, darling. (*Kisses him.*) See you in three weeks.

(*Enter* SPRULES *through double doors.*)

Yes, clear away, Sprules.

(*Exit* LOUISE *through double doors.*)

(AUBREY *comes down singing—catches sight of* SPRULES *standing up* R.C.)

AUBREY. Oh, Sprules—— (*Seeing* SPRULES *staring at him.*) What's the matter, man?

SPRULES. You're looking a little pale, sir.

AUBREY. I'm feeling a little pale. I've got a wonderful idea, Sprules.

SPRULES. Yes, sir?

(SIMPSON *enters with tray through double doors, helps* SPRULES *to clear the breakfast things from table.* AUBREY C.; SPRULES *top of table;* SIMPSON *on* R. *of table.*)

AUBREY. And I'm going down to my workshop to experiment.

SPRULES. Yes, sir.

AUBREY. I mustn't on any account be disturbed, Sprules.

SPRULES. I'll see that you're not, sir.

AUBREY. You see, I'm working on some very high explosives, Sprules.

SPRULES. Yes, sir.
AUBREY. Frightfully high explosives, Sprules. So high that if they exploded you'd never find a bit of me again.
SPRULES. Very good, sir.
AUBREY. In fact Sprules, they're so high that I'd rather nobody left the house till I've finished.
SPRULES. Yes, sir.

(*After* SIMPSON *has cleared the breakfast things, she exits through double doors.*)

AUBREY. That will be, say—(*looks at his watch*)—say twelve o'clock, Sprules.
SPRULES. Yes, sir. (*Removes white cloth from table.*)
AUBREY. Of course, it wouldn't matter if I was killed.
SPRULES. No, sir.
AUBREY. What!
SPRULES (*injured*). No, sir, but——

(*Enter* MISS MULLETT *through double doors, comes down to* AUBREY C. *on his* R.)

MISS MULLETT. Oh, I was looking for you, Aubrey.
AUBREY. I'm just going down to my workshop, auntie. (*Going up* C.)
MISS MULLETT. I'll come with you. (*Moves after him.*)
AUBREY (*quickly*). Oh, no, no, no!
MISS MULLETT. And why not, pray?
AUBREY (*bringing her down stage*). You can come—er—after twelve o'clock. Not a moment before. I've got some frightfully dangerous work on and I wouldn't have anyone near me. (*Business of arm round her neck and squeezing her chin.*)
MISS MULLETT. Very well, have it your own way. (*Goes to chair* R. *Sits down and begins knitting.*)
AUBREY. And, Sprules, if any of my creditors call, tell them to come round again—after twelve! After twelve, Sprules, don't forget.

(*Exit* AUBREY *into garden through French windows to* R.)

MISS MULLETT. Where's Giles, Sprules?
SPRULES (*taking table up* L. *behind settle*). I don't know, ma'am; shall I find him for you?
MISS MULLETT. What?
SPRULES. I say, shall I find him for you? (*Moves chair at* R.C. *to table* L.C.)
MISS MULLETT. Don't shout, man! I'm not deaf!
SPRULES (*moves* LOUISE'S *chair up to* L. *of clock*). Can I give him a message for you, ma'am?

Miss Mullett. No, it doesn't matter; I told him to bring me a cucumber so that I can make the salad for lunch. (*Looks at her watch.*)

(*Enter* Simpson *at double doors with telegram, glances at* Sprules *who is by clock, with an aside* "Where's master?")

(*Enter* Giles *with cucumber through French windows.*)

Yes, Simpson?

Simpson. Telegram for the master, ma'am.

(*Exit* Sprules *through double doors.*)

Miss Mullett. Well, give it to me. I'm going down to the workshop in a few minutes, and I'll give it to him. (Simpson *comes to her and gives telegram.*)

Giles (*on steps of window*). Cucumber!

Miss Mullett. Oh, there you are, Giles—you're late.

(*Exit* Simpson *through double doors.*)

Giles (*up stage, looking at clock*). I ain't late—you said twelve o'clock—ain't twelve o'clock.

Miss Mullett. That clock's slow. (*Goes on knitting.*)

Giles. You needn't shout, 'm—I ain't deaf!

(Giles *puts clock on to twelve o'clock.*)

Miss Mullett (*speaking under her breath*). Oh, what impudence —impertinent——

(*Enter* Louise *through double doors.*)

Louise. Ah, there you are, auntie! (*Coming down to her.*)

Miss Mullett (*still seated* R.). Louise, here's a telegram for Aubrey, my dear—shall I take it?

Louise (R.C.). No, no! Not yet, because——

Giles. Please, 'm, I—— (L.C.)

Louise. One minute, Giles—— (*To* Miss Mullett.) Aubrey mustn't be disturbed, auntie, until——

(Giles *goes to table and places the cucumber with the eggs and flowers.*)

Miss Mullett. Until what, my dear?

Louise. Until twelve o'clock, auntie!

Miss Mullett. It is twelve o'clock now, dear.

Louise. What! (*Turns round and looks at clock.*) Why, so it is. (*Goes across to speaking-tube.*)

Giles. Please, 'm—— (*Trying to get a word in.*)

Louise. Do be quiet a minute, Giles. (*Gives a violent blow down speaking-tube and stands listening. To* Giles.) Now, what is it?

GILES. Oh, I only wanted to tell you, 'm, just put that clock on ten minutes.

LOUISE. What!!! *(She drops speaking-tube and stands gazing at* GILES *in horror.)*

(A tremendous explosion is heard off R.)

MISS MULLETT. Gracious! What's that? *(Jumps up.)*
LOUISE. It's the workshop—and Aubrey's there!

(MISS MULLETT, GILES *and* LOUISE *rush wildly to French windows.* SPRULES *and* SIMPSON *rush on from double doors shouting and screaming. They all make for the garden, but debris from explosion, bricks, tiles, fragments of plaster, etc., is falling, preventing them from going that way.* SPRULES, *waving his arms about wildly, ushers them back through double doors, shouting :)*

SPRULES. Giles! Giles! Simpson! Save yourselves!

(They all rush out through double doors, leaving LOUISE *in mental agony. She thinks* AUBREY *has been blown up.)*

(Smoke is seen through French windows—check lights on back cloth slightly.)

(LOUISE *walks slowly down* R., *sinks into arm-chair.*)

LOUISE. I've killed him, I've killed him.

(At that moment AUBREY *appears from French windows* R., *his face is blackened with gunpowder, his clothes are hanging on him in shreds, he gazes wildly around as he staggers on to* C. *of stage and collapses on settle* L.)

CURTAIN.

ACT II

SCENE.—*Same as before. The table used for tea is set up stage* L. *to open, and one small chair—another small chair is set by the clock, and one on* R. *of table* L.C.)

TIME.—*Three weeks have elapsed.* (*Afternoon.*)

(*At rise of the* CURTAIN, LOUISE *is discovered lying on the settle; she is reading a novel, she is in deep mourning, but her attitude shows complete indifference, and she is laughing over her book. After a slight pause* SPRULES *enters from double doors* R.; *the moment she hears him she sits up, puts her book away and sighs heavily.*)

SPRULES (*up* R.C.). Mr. George Maitland is on the 'phone, madam.

(LOUISE *rises and is going towards doors* R., SPRULES *indicating 'phone on table.*)

I've put you through.

(LOUISE *turns back to table* L.C. *to 'phone and picks up receiver.*)

LOUISE. Hello! Yes, Mrs. Allington speaking.

(SPRULES *is still lingering at double doors, hoping to hear the conversation.* LOUISE *looks at him.*)

(*He exits.*)

(*When the door closes her voice and expression must change.*)

Yes, yes, is that you, Aubrey darling? . . . All right, I'll call you George. (*Laughing.*) I must get used to it. Everything all right? . . . You'll be down in half an hour, good! . . . But it's deadly dull being a widow. Where are you now? . . . Reading—they couldn't bury you, Aubrey, because they couldn't find anything of you to bury. (*Laughing.*) Oh yes, all in black. . . . Oh, Aubrey, I mean George, I wish there was some way I could be sure of recognizing you when you come in, what? . . . You'll be singing—oh, Aubrey, I never knew you had a voice. (*Laughing.*) All right, dear, you shall have the room next to mine.

(SPRULES *has entered through double doors, and stands listening.* LOUISE *changes her tone again.*)

Then I'll expect you in half an hour, Mr. Maitland. Good-bye. (*Hangs up receiver.*)

SPRULES (*crossing at back to* L.). I suppose Mr. Maitland will have the spare room, ma'am ? (*Takes small gate-leg table from front of bookcase* L.C.)
LOUISE. Er—no, Sprules. I think you'd better put him in the blue room.
SPRULES (*surprised; stopping* C. *with table*). The one next to yours, ma'am ?
LOUISE. Yes, I think so. It's a more attractive room.
SPRULES. Very good, ma'am. (*Sets table down* C.)

(*Enter* SIMPSON *through double doors, with tea things, places them on cabinet by clock.* LOUISE *crosses to her.*)

LOUISE. Has Miss Everard arrived yet ?
SIMPSON. Not yet, ma'am.
LOUISE. It's quite time she was here. I think I'll walk down and meet her.

(*Exit* LOUISE *French windows to* L.)

SPRULES (*waits till she has disappeared. To* SIMPSON). Now what does she want to put him in the room next to hers for ?
SIMPSON (*up* R.C.). Who's " him " ?
SPRULES (L.C. *at table*). Mr. Maitland.
SIMPSON. Well, why shouldn't she ? (*Takes tablecloth from drawer of cabinet.*)

(SPRULES *beckons to her mysteriously, she comes down to him.*
SIMPSON R.C. ; SPRULES L.C.)

SPRULES. Who do you think is coming here this afternoon ?
SIMPSON (*puzzled*). Why, Mr. George Maitland, of course.
SPRULES. Mr. George Maitland don't exist—he's dead.
SIMPSON. Well, if 'e's dead, 'ow can 'e be coming 'ere to-day ?
SPRULES. He isn't—but *she* thinks he is. (*Looks round to see they are not overheard.*)
SIMPSON. Wot on earth are you drivin' at, Mr. Sprules ?
SPRULES. Listen ! The poor guv'nor being dead, the money goes to his cousin, George Maitland of Mexico.
SIMPSON. 'Ow do you know ?
SPRULES. 'Cos I've seen it in the will. I come across it in the drawer after the poor master's death, so I took the liberty of reading it.
SIMPSON. Well ?
SPRULES. Now, I happens to know too, that George Maitland of Mexico is dead, but they've never had actual proof of his death, so they've advertised for him. (*Looking round,* L. *and* R. *at back, makes certain no one is about.*)
SIMPSON. Yes ?
SPRULES (*comes down stage to* L. *of* SIMPSON). Well, I says to

myself: "Sprules," I says, "it's a lot of money it is, and you want to get married..."

SIMPSON (*coyly*). Oh, Mr. Sprules. (*Toying with tea-cloth, corner of which she is biting.*)

SPRULES. Don't fidget with that thing! (*He snatches the tea-cloth away and puts it on table.*) "But George Maitland is dead, so he can never get it."

SIMPSON (*puzzled*). Go on.

SPRULES. But if someone exactly like him came along and said: "I'm George Maitland from Mexico, and I claim that money"— they'd have to brass up. (*Goes up to cabinet* R. *for tray.*)

SIMPSON (*up* C., *breathlessly*). So you've got someone to dress up as George Maitland, and it's him who's coming here to-day.

SPRULES (*goes to double doors, tray in hand*). You've got it.

SIMPSON (*eagerly, up* C. *following a little*). Who is he?

SPRULES (*placing tray on sideboard for a moment, makes certain the doors are closed, picks it up again, comes down and brings* SIMPSON *forward*). My brother Henery.

SIMPSON. What, him who's at Drury Lane; then that's why he came to see you yesterday.

SPRULES. That's right—I had to prime him up and show him the photo of the real George Maitland so that he could know what to make up like. (*Places tray on tea-table.*) If this comes off it means tons of money for us.

SIMPSON (*coyly*). Then—we shall be able to get married, Mr. Sprules.

SPRULES (*comes* C. *and places his arm round* SIMPSON'S *waist*). Yes, and we can clear away to a nice little country cottage, and no one will be any the wiser. (*Kisses her.*)

SIMPSON. Have you fixed it all up?

SPRULES. I've put my brother through his paces.

SIMPSON. And he's coming here to-day as George Maitland.

SPRULES. Yes, he got the wind up about it, but I told him it was as easy as falling off a log. He was on the telephone to the mistress just now; as a matter of fact, *I arranged for him to come to-morrow*, but he must have changed his mind.

SIMPSON (R.). What's he like?

SPRULES (L.). You can't mistake him, he's got a brown beard and moustache—he'll announce himself as George Maitland—and I've arranged that if we want to warn him to signal like this. Number one—(*business scratching elbow*) that means—be careful. Number two—(*business rubbing ear*) that means—danger, and number three—(*business rubbing nose and making a clicking noise with mouth*) come into the kitchen.

(SIMPSON *imitates him.*)

Don't make that noise.

SIMPSON. You did it.

SPRULES. Yes, I know, but I am trying to explain things to you, and if we can't catch his eye, we've got to drop something, so as to draw his attention, like this—— (*Business of pretending to drop tray on table.*)

SIMPSON. If it's very important?

SPRULES. Yes, not otherwise. (*Places a chair from up* L. *at* R. *of table.*)

SIMPSON (*admiringly, sitting on the chair* R. *of table*). You have got a wonderful brain, Mr. Sprules.

SPRULES (*proudly*). A good butler is like a patent medicine—there's nothing he can't do. (*Kiss.*)

(*Both laugh*—MISS MULLETT *enters through double doors—they suddenly become grave.*)

MISS MULLETT (*coming down* R.). Where's your mistress?

SIMPSON. She's just gone out to meet Miss Everard, ma'am.

(*Exit* SIMPSON *through double doors.*)

MISS MULLETT. What!

SPRULES (C., *loudly*). She's just gone out to meet Miss Everard, ma'am.

MISS MULLETT. You needn't shout, I'm not deaf.

(GILES *is seen to enter from* R. *of terrace, followed by* MISS JEAN EVERARD *and* MRS. ALLINGTON. JEAN EVERARD *is a distinctly pretty woman of about 28. She is very smartly dressed in travelling costume.* MRS. ALLINGTON *leans on her arm and speaks very sadly and feebly.*)

JEAN (*as they descend steps of window*). He keeps the garden beautifully. (GILES *disappears* L.)

LOUISE. Yes, dear, but he's a terrible nuisance, he's always having trouble with cook. (*To* SPRULES.) Sprules, go and see about Miss Everard's luggage.

SPRULES (*crossing at back*). Yes, ma'am.

(*Exit* SPRULES *through double doors.*)

MISS MULLETT. I was just asking after you, Louise.

LOUISE. Auntie, this is Miss Everard—my aunt, Miss Mullett.

(JEAN *and* MISS MULLETT *shake hands.*)

Miss Everard is an old friend of mine, auntie.

(MISS MULLETT R.C.; JEAN C.; LOUISE L.C.)

JEAN (*to* MISS MULLETT). I simply had to come down and see her, Miss Mullett. Poor Louise.

Miss Mullett (r.). It's a most deplorable business . . . (*Sitting* r.)

(Louise *takes out handkerchief, sobbing.*)

Jean (*turning to her*). There, there, darling, don't cry!
Louise (l.). Poor darling Aubrey!
Jean (c.). Such a sudden end, too!
Louise. Yes, ten minutes before he expected it.
Jean. What, darling?
Louise. I said—so unexpected. (*Goes to settle and sits.*)
Jean (*to* Miss Mullett). I suppose—er—nothing was found of him?
Miss Mullett. What?
Jean. I say, "Nothing was found of him."
Miss Mullett. You needn't shout—I'm not deaf.
Louise (*tearfully*). They found a trouser b-b-button, but they weren't sure whether it was his or Sprules', apparently they both went to the same t-tailor. (*Bus. putting away handkerchief.*)

(Miss Mullett *begins knitting.*)

Jean. My dear, I had rather a shock to-day. (*Sits near* Louise *on settle up stage end.*)
Louise. Really, dear?
Jean. Yes, just now, I thought I saw my husband.
Louise. Jean, I never knew you were married.
Jean. I know, I never told you. You see my husband is dead.
Louise. Oh, my darling! But your name?
Jean. Oh, yes, you see George and I were married secretly, we were just going to announce our marriage when George was called to Mexico on urgent business.
Louise. Oh, I see!
Jean. I never saw him again.
Louise. Never saw him again?
Jean. No, I heard later that he had been shot.
Louise (*startled*). Shot!
Jean (*proudly*). He gave his life for another.
Louise. Oh! How heroic of him.
Jean (*sighing*). I knew he was a hero when he married me; poor dear George, from the day he met me he never looked at another girl.
Louise. How wonderful!
Jean. Of course, if one can really trust one's husband——
Louise. Oh, I know I trusted Aubrey implicitly, but not out of my sight. But to-day, darling, what happened to-day?
Jean. Oh, yes, of course! I was sitting in my compartment when a man got in. I was reading my paper, and I shouldn't have

looked up, only he started humming a tune that dear George used to love when we were first married—I can't remember the name of it, but it went like this. (*Sings to the tune of "Ta-ra-ra-boom-de-ay."*)

LOUISE. I seem to have heard that tune somewhere. (*Sings.*) De-de-de-de-de-de. It's out of one of the Gilbert and Sullivan Operas, I think.

MISS MULLETT. Would you mind doing that again ?

(JEAN *and* LOUISE *sing together*—MISS MULLETT *joining in.*)

I know! It's out of one of the oratorios.

JEAN. I rather think it is, Miss Mullett. (*To* LOUISE.) At any rate, it gave me quite a shock. Then suddenly he turned round—and, darling, it was my husband to the life.

LOUISE. Good heavens—what did you do ?

JEAN. I said " George ! " (*falls back*)—just like that. And then I think I fainted.

MISS MULLETT. Why !

LOUISE. The shock, auntie, of course.

MISS MULLETT. What shock ?

LOUISE (*aside*). Oh, dear, oh, dear ! (*Aloud.*) Miss Everard . . .

MISS MULLETT. Don't shout, dear, it's all right.

LOUISE. Miss Everard thought she saw her husband.

MISS MULLETT. Is she married ?

LOUISE. Yes.

MISS MULLETT. Is he enough to make her faint ?

LOUISE. No, no, no ! But he's dead.

MISS MULLETT (*finally*). Well, if he's dead, she couldn't have seen him.

(LOUISE *gives a movement to indicate to* JEAN *how hopeless it is to continue.*)

LOUISE (*to* MISS EVERARD). Darling, did you see him again ?

JEAN. No; when I came to, he'd completely disappeared.

LOUISE. But didn't you ask the officials ?

JEAN. Yes, but they hadn't seen anybody.

LOUISE. How extraordinary !

MISS MULLETT. What's extraordinary ?

LOUISE. We're still talking of Miss Everard's husband, auntie.

MISS MULLETT. But I thought you said he was dead ?

LOUISE. So he is. He is ! He is ! . . . but . . . (*Gives a helpless gesture.*) Jean, you don't think you could have been mistaken ?

JEAN. Dear, I'd know George anywhere.

LOUISE. What's he like ?

JEAN. Well, he's got a . . .

(*Enter* SPRULES *through double doors, standing* L. *of them.*)

SPRULES. Mr. Chesterman, ma'am.

(*Enter* CHESTERMAN *through double doors. Enter* SIMPSON *double doors, with teapot, comes down at back to top of table, places teapot on it.*)

LOUISE (*rises*). How do you do, Mr. Chesterman? (*Shakes hands, meeting* CHESTERMAN C.) Miss Mullett I think you know.

(*Exit* SPRULES *through double doors.*)

Jean, this is Mr. Chesterman—Miss Everard.

(*They bow.*)

Will you have some tea?

(JEAN L. *on settle;* MISS MULLETT R.; CHESTERMAN R.C.; LOUISE C.; SIMPSON L.C.)

CHESTERMAN. I've had a wire from your late husband's cousin, Mrs. Allington, and he's coming down here to call on you.

LOUISE. Yes, I'm expecting him here to-day. (*Sits chair* R. *of table, pours out tea.*)

CHESTERMAN. Really?

LOUISE. He rang me up to say he was coming down.

JEAN. I'm quite looking forward to seeing him.

(CHESTERMAN *goes and stands behind table ready to hand round tea. Exit* SIMPSON *through double doors.*)

CHESTERMAN. Of course you know—Mrs. Allington, that owing to the sad death of your poor husband—— (*Handing plate of bread and butter to* JEAN.)

LOUISE. Poor dear Aubrey! (*Bus. of pretending to wipe her eyes with handkerchief.*)

CHESTERMAN. You now become entitled to the whole of the money at the death of the present heir George Maitland. (*Cross to* MISS MULLETT R., *hands her cup of tea.*)

LOUISE (*amazed*). I do?

CHESTERMAN. You do. (*Going to his original position behind tea-table.*)

LOUISE. But—you never told me.

CHESTERMAN. I left you a copy of the will.

LOUISE. Yes, but my husband couldn't understand it.

CHESTERMAN. I have often heard such remarks.

LOUISE. I wish Aubrey had known that before.

CHESTERMAN. I beg your pardon.

(MISS MULLETT R.; CHESTERMAN *behind tea-table.* LOUISE *sitting* R. *of table;* JEAN *sitting* L. *of table, on settle.*)

LOUISE (*hurriedly*). I mean he would have—er—it would have comforted him to know that I was—er—provided for.

JEAN. It would have made a difference to him.

LOUISE. Oh, it would have made a great difference to him!

MISS MULLETT. What would have made a difference to whom?

LOUISE. We were talking of poor Aubrey's cousin, auntie.

MISS MULLETT. What's he done?

LOUISE. Nothing, auntie, but Mr. Chesterman was saying that at his death . . .

MISS MULLETT. What, is he dead too

LOUISE. No; but when he *does* die . . . (*Hands tea to* CHESTERMAN, *who hands it to* JEAN.)

MISS MULLETT. Who says he's going to die?

LOUISE (*louder*). No one, auntie; but if he was dead the money would come to me.

(LOUISE *makes a gesture to the others to signify the hopelessness of continuing.* MISS MULLETT *rises, hands cup and saucer to* CHESTERMAN, *who meets her* C., *and makes movement towards double doors.*)

MISS MULLETT. Why you want to imagine Aubrey's cousin's going to die, I don't know. He may live for years!

(*Exit through double doors.*)

(CHESTERMAN *places empty cup and saucer on tea-tray and takes his cup of tea and goes down* R.)

CHESTERMAN. I'm sorry to say, Mrs. Allington, that your husband's estate is working out worse than we thought.

LOUISE. Poor dear fellow! He was always so generous to me.

JEAN. Was he, darling?

LOUISE. Yes—he gave me everything credit could buy. (*Handkerchief to eyes.*)

JEAN (*consolingly*). Dear, you must try and be brave.

(CHESTERMAN *sits in* MISS MULLETT'S *chair* R.)

LOUISE. Y-y-yes!

JEAN. Remember you have a part to play now.

LOUISE. I—I have!

(CHESTERMAN R.; LOUISE C. *in chair* R. *of table*; JEAN L.)

JEAN. He would want you to play it well!

LOUISE. He said so!

JEAN. I speak as one widow to another. (*Sobbing.*)

(*In the garden a man's voice is heard singing—*" *Ta-ra-ra-ra-boom-de-ay.*" *All rise.*)

(LOUISE *rises with a smile, not noticing* JEAN, *who is transfixed with amazement.* LOUISE *walks briskly across to* R.)

LOUISE. Who's this?

(JEAN *goes down* L.; CHESTERMAN *by fireplace;* LOUISE *down* R. *behind* MISS MULLETT'S *chair*.)

(AUBREY ALLINGTON *appears at French windows. He is disguised as* GEORGE MAITLAND, *wears a brown suit, has a beard and moustache, rather tanned. He wears an extravagant Mexican hat and speaks with an assumed Yankee twang*.)

AUBREY. Hullo, folks! (*Up stage at window*.) Say! can I drift in? (*Comes down stage*.) And whom have I the honour to address?
LOUISE. I'm your cousin Louise Allington.
AUBREY (*taking her hand*). Vibrate that again, sweetie.
LOUISE. I'm your cousin Louise Allington.
AUBREY. I'm real glad to meet you socially.

(*They shake hands. He removes large hat*.)

Registered! (*Puts hat on floor near settle*.)

(JEAN *has risen*.)

I'm your long-lost cousin George Maitland from Mexico.

(CHESTERMAN *at fire*—LOUISE R.C.—AUBREY C.—JEAN L.)

(JEAN *then rushes at* AUBREY, *flings her arms round his neck and faints in his arms.* AUBREY *lays her down on the settle.* LOUISE *must express in her face, the realization of the whole situation*.)

She's fainted—get some water.

(CHESTERMAN *shouting* "Water" *rushes out through double doors*.)

(*Aside*.) Quick, what does this mean?
LOUISE (*aside*). You met her at the station to-day?

(AUBREY *has picked up the teapot absent-mindedly and allows tea to come out of spout on to the carpet*.)

AUBREY (*aside*). I know, and she shrieked out "George," so I bolted.
LOUISE (*aside*). She's George Maitland's wife!
AUBREY (*aside*). I can see that, but what am I to do?
LOUISE (*aside*). Play up to it—pretend you are her husband. Do what you like, only give me time to think it out. Hush!

(CHESTERMAN *enters through double doors with a glass of water*.)

AUBREY (*takes glass*). Thank you so much. (*Sprinkling* JEAN.) That's all right now—she'll be herself again in a minute.

(LOUISE *takes glass of water from* AUBREY, *goes to back of settle, round its end, gives* JEAN *water*.)

(JEAN *gradually revives.*)

CHESTERMAN (R., *advancing to* AUBREY). A terrible shock, naturally. (*Smiling.*) I must congratulate you doubly.

AUBREY (R.C.). Thank you.

CHESTERMAN. You never expected a fortune and a wife on the same day.

AUBREY. I didn't.

CHESTERMAN. Didn't you?

AUBREY. No, I didn't.

CHESTERMAN. It's a day you'll never forget.

AUBREY. It is.

JEAN (*almost revived*). Where's George? (*Looks round.*)

(LOUISE *signs to* AUBREY, *takes glass from* JEAN *and puts it on table.*)

AUBREY. Here I am—darling! (*Crosses to* JEAN, *sits on settle with her down stage end.*)

JEAN. I'm—I'm better now. George—George—is it really you?

AUBREY (*stands up as he speaks*). Y-y-yes, d-darling! It's m-m-me all right.

(LOUISE *sitting behind settle again, looking on.* CHESTERMAN *down* R.)

JEAN. Oh, George!

(JEAN *throws her arms around his neck—he loses his balance and falls into her arms on settle.*)

(*Faintly.*) It is really you, George, isn't it?

AUBREY. Oh, yes, darling—it's nobody else.

JEAN (*gazing at him*). Yes, I'm sure it is.

AUBREY. I'm certain of it, too.

JEAN. George—kiss me.

(JEAN *and* AUBREY *kiss.*)

(*Sighing.*) I could have told you anywhere, George, by the way you kiss.

(AUBREY, *after kissing* JEAN, *appears to rather enjoy the situation.*)

AUBREY. It seems almost too good to be true.

(LOUISE *still behind settle.*)

LOUISE (*coldly*). It does.

AUBREY. Just like a dream, eh?

LOUISE. Oh, you will wake up in a minute. (*Slightly forward to* AUDREY *down stage end of settle.*)

JEAN. To think of the years we have lost, George!

AUBREY. Oh, I know all about that, darling, think of what lies before us. (*Rises. Moves* C.)

Louise (*pointedly*). Yes, I should think of that. (*Down* L.)

(AUBREY *gives a slight start*.)

(*Enter* SPRULES *through double doors. The moment he sees* AUBREY, *he begins making signs—scratching elbow.* AUBREY *gazes at* SPRULES *in amazement.* LOUISE *also sees* SPRULES.)

(CHESTERMAN R.; SPRULES *up* R.C.; AUBREY C.; JEAN L.C. LOUISE L.)

(*Coming* L.C.) Sprules, what on earth are you doing? (AUBREY *crosses* L. *shaking his head as though he does not understand* SPRULES.)

SPRULES. N-n-nothing, madam.

LOUISE. Well, don't go on like that, please. I don't like it. What do you want?

SPRULES. Which room am I to put Mr. Maitland in, madam?

LOUISE. The Blue Room, Sprules—the one next to mine.

JEAN (*coyly*). Oh, no, darling, not now!

(SPRULES *makes more signs to* AUBREY—*ear sign*.)

(*Rising and coming* L.C. *to* LOUISE.) Hadn't we better tell Sprules that George—that I—oh, help me out, dear. (*Turns away bashfully*.)

(CHESTERMAN R.; SPRULES R.C.; LOUISE C.; JEAN L.C.; AUBREY L.)

LOUISE (*desperately*). Sprules—Mr. George Maitland turns out to be—to be Miss Everard's husband——

(SPRULES *shows surprise*.)

Yes, it *is* a surprise to all of us!

JEAN (*smiling*). So you see, Sprules, you will take Mr. Maitland's things to my room and——

(AUBREY *takes cake dish from* L., *of table, unconsciously offers* JEAN *a cake*.)

LOUISE. But, Jean, it's only got a—a—(*desperately*)—single—it's *quite* a *small* room.

(SPRULES *endeavours to be friendly on catching* AUBREY'S *eye.* CHESTERMAN *smiles and turns up to window, then down* R. *again*.)

JEAN (*sweetly*). Oh, but we shan't mind that, shall we, George?

AUBREY (*cheerfully*). Not a bit—darling. (*Embrace*.) What is enough for one is enough for two!

(SPRULES *makes the ear sign*.)

LOUISE (*icily*). Oh, of course, if you don't mind——

AUBREY. As if we should!

JEAN. That's all right, then, Sprules. (*Crosses* LOUISE *to* C.)

(CHESTERMAN *down* R.—SPRULES R.C.—JEAN C.—LOUISE L.C.—
AUBREY L.)

SPRULES. V-v-very good, ma'am. (*Turns up stage towards doors and gives* AUBREY *nose sign.*)

(AUBREY *turns and looks towards* SPRULES, *sees* SPRULES *making signs—very puzzled—takes up lid of muffin-dish and uses it as a hand mirror.*)

(*Exit* SPRULES *through double doors.*)

JEAN. I think, George, I'll go upstairs—(*goes up* C., *turns to* AUBREY)—and rest for a little. (*Looks lovingly at him.*) Would you like to take me up, darling?

AUBREY. Of course I will—dearest!

(CHESTERMAN R.—JEAN C.—LOUISE L.C.—AUBREY L.)

(AUBREY *crosses to* JEAN C.)

LOUISE (*as* AUBREY *passes*). Oh, I'll pay you out for this.

(JEAN *and* AUBREY *kiss.*)

(*Exit through double doors, and go up staircase arm-in-arm.*)

(LOUISE *down* L., CHESTERMAN *down* R., *both looking after* JEAN *and* AUBREY.)

CHESTERMAN (*at fireplace*). What a charming picture!

LOUISE. Very! (*Through these lines she must show she is boiling over with rage. She goes up and closes double doors.*)

CHESTERMAN. We little knew what we were doing when we brought him down, did we?

LOUISE. We didn't!

CHESTERMAN. He's a singularly fascinating man. I can see any woman falling in love with him.

LOUISE. Can you? (*Coming down to tea-table* C.)

CHESTERMAN. But one can see he's madly in love with her.

LOUISE. Really!

CHESTERMAN. Oh, it's obvious! They're just like lovers. I'm afraid you'll find it very dull just now, Mrs. Allington.

LOUISE. Dull—why? (*Drinking glass of water.*)

CHESTERMAN (R.). He'll monopolize her altogether now.

LOUISE (L., *firmly*). Will he? (*Sits* L. *of tea-table on settle.*)

(*Enter* GILES, *stands at French windows with basket of gooseberries.*)

CHESTERMAN. And you'll have to look on.
GILES. Like a few gooseberries?
LOUISE. No, thank you, Giles.
GILES. The berries are very fine.

LOUISE. No, nothing, thank you.
GILES. All right, 'm.

(GILES *exits* L. *French windows.*)

LOUISE (*to* CHESTERMAN). You must excuse our gardener coming in here—he's not on speaking terms with cook.

CHESTERMAN. Still, at least you've been the means of bringing two other people together. Think how nice it will be for you in the years to come to be able, perhaps, to tell their children that——

(*Re-enter* AUBREY *double doors; comes down* C. LOUISE *on settle.* CHESTERMAN R.)

Ah, here is the new bridegroom! Well, Mr. Maitland, there's no need to ask if you are happy—your face tells its own tale! Ha, ha!

AUBREY (*grimly*). Ha, ha!

LOUISE (*icily*). Mr. Chesterman was just saying that you and your—your wife, Mr. Maitland, are like lovers. (*Rises and goes down* L.)

AUBREY. Ha, ha! You think that, do you?

CHESTERMAN (R.C., *digging him jocularly and turning away* R.). Of course I do, you lucky dog!

AUBREY (*laughing*). That's funny, Mrs. Allington, isn't it? (*Attempts to kick* CHESTERMAN *from behind.*)

LOUISE (*gravely*). Screamingly funny!

CHESTERMAN (*putting out hand to shake hands*). Well, I'm afraid I must be running away.

AUBREY (*eagerly*). Oh, do stop and have a cup of cocoa, or have a bovril—I mean, I'm sure Mrs. Allington would be delighted if you would.

(CHESTERMAN R.; AUBREY C.; LOUISE L.)

CHESTERMAN. I'm sorry, but I'm afraid I can't. (*Looks at his watch.*) It's later than I thought. (*Crosses to* LOUISE.) Good-bye, Mrs. Allington—(*shakes hands*)—good-bye, Mr. Maitland. (*With a jovial smile.*) You're done for this time.

(*Exit* CHESTERMAN *through double doors.*)

AUBREY. I believe you're right. (*Goes up after* CHESTERMAN— *closes doors and returns.*)

(*There is a little pause during which* AUBREY *regards* LOUISE *nervously.*)

LOUISE (*angrily; down* L.). Now, Aubrey, perhaps you'll explain your conduct.

AUBREY. *My* conduct! (*Coming down, sits in chair by fireplace.*)

LOUISE. Yes, your " darling this " and " darling that." (*Coming over* R.)

AUBREY (*annoyed*). I like that!

LOUISE. Well, I don't; and what's more, I'm not going to have it.

AUBREY. Oh, don't be so silly.

LOUISE (*sarcastically*). "What is enough for one is enough for two," you—you—Mormon! (*Going* L.)

AUBREY. Merely a little corroborative detail. (*Rises and comes* C.)

LOUISE. Corroborative fiddlesticks! And taking her up to her room, too! (*Coming a little* C. *towards* AUBREY.)

AUBREY. Oh, that's nothing!

LOUISE. If you do that to-day, what on earth are you going to do to-morrow. (*Crosses* AUBREY *to* R.)

AUBREY. You told me to. (*Goes to tea-table, then sits on settle.*)

LOUISE (*furiously*). Told you to! (*Going to him.*) How dare you!

(AUBREY *rises and retreats to down stage end of settle.*)

How dare you!

(AUBREY *retreats further to back of chair extreme* L.)

How dare you!

AUBREY (*sullenly*). I couldn't help myself.

LOUISE. Couldn't help yourself! You had an enormous helping and you enjoyed it——

AUBREY. It was your suggestion. (*Crosses* R.)

LOUISE (C.). What?

AUBREY. You said I was to play it up for all I was worth. (*Crosses* L. *and sits on settle.*)

LOUISE. That's right! Now say it's my fault. (*Sits beside him on settle.*)

AUBREY. It *is* your fault. You made me die, but I didn't want to do it. (*Rises.*)

LOUISE. How was I to know *she* was going to turn up?

AUBREY (*goes* C.). You weren't to know any more than I was. It's just happened. (*Sitting at tea-table* C.)

LOUISE. Well, it's got to unhappen!

AUBREY. I don't see how. (*Rise, cross down* R.) She's got first call on me, in the eyes of the Law.

LOUISE (*startled*). Aubrey, what do you mean?

AUBREY (*calmly*). What I say. (*Sits on arm of chair by fireplace.*)

LOUISE. I am your lawful wedded wife.

AUBREY (*rising*). Pardon me—you're a corpse's relic. (*Carelessly.*) I am George Maitland, of Mexico, sole heir to four hundred and seventy thousand dollars, owing to the unfortunate demise of my dear cousin, Aubrey Maitland Allington.

LOUISE. You're nothing of the kind—you're my husband. (*Rises. Crosses to* AUBREY.)

AUBREY (*airily*). Oh, no! Oh, no! My legal better half is at the present moment reclining on her couch upstairs planning golden dreams for our second honeymoon. 'Ra! 'ra! 'ra!

LOUISE. Oh, it's intolerable! (*Goes to* AUBREY *and clings to him speaking very tearfully.*) Aubrey, you don't mean it—you can't mean it! You wouldn't desert me for that—that—Jezebel! (*Sobs.*)

(AUBREY *goes up to the window to see that they are not overlooked, then goes down to* LOUISE *and embraces her.*)

AUBREY. I don't want to desert you. (*Kiss.*) But what's to be done?

LOUISE. Oh, there *must* be some way out!

(AUBREY *takes her hand and leads her to settle.*)

AUBREY (*sits down stage of* LOUISE *on settle*). Well, let's sit down and talk it over.

(*They both sit, deep in thought.*)

LOUISE. Aubrey, I've got an idea.

AUBREY. I suppose you want me to die again?

LOUISE. However did you guess?

AUBREY (*groans*). Guess! You've got a mind like a burial service.

LOUISE. Listen, dear! (*Sits closer to* AUBREY.) Chesterman was saying this afternoon that at Cousin George's death the money all comes to me.

AUBREY (*amazed*). What!

LOUISE. Yes, it all comes to me.

AUBREY. Why the dickens didn't he say so before?

LOUISE. That's just what I told him. He said he left you a copy of the will.

AUBREY. I need never have turned up as George Maitland.

LOUISE. Of course not.

AUBREY. Oh! I'm not at all sure I haven't an action against him—for inciting me to murder myself.

LOUISE. Never mind that! Darling, all you've got to do is to die again.

AUBREY. I'm sick of dying.

LOUISE (*laughing*). You did look so funny, Aubrey, when you came in with your face all black.

AUBREY. I didn't feel funny!

LOUISE (*putting her arm round* AUBREY). You will die, darling, won't you, just to please me.

AUBREY. It all depends.

LOUISE. The moment you're dead, you know, the money is mine absolutely.

AUBREY. Absolutely.

LOUISE. Yes, Chesterman told me so to-day.
AUBREY (*laughing*). I say—she'll—(*pointing upstairs*)—be a real widow then.
LOUISE (*laughing*). Serve her right.

(LOUISE *and* AUBREY *burst out laughing and embrace affectionately.*)

(SIMPSON *enters through double doors, stops horror-struck, and they spring apart.*)

AUBREY. And the animal hugged him just like that. (*Crossing* R.) It's a terrible thing the buffalo hug.

(SIMPSON *up* R.C. *signs to* AUBREY *scratching elbow.*)

LOUISE. What is it, Simpson?
SIMPSON. I was just going to clear away the tea, madam.
LOUISE. You'd like some tea, George?
AUBREY. Yes, I'll have a tankard. (R.)
LOUISE. Bring some fresh tea, Simpson.

(*They do not take any further notice of* SIMPSON, *who comes to table watching them, takes up teapot and muffin dish—she deliberately throws muffin dish on floor.* AUBREY *and* LOUISE *turn sharply.*)

Good gracious, Simpson, what are you doing?
SIMPSON. Beg pardon, ma'am, but it *slipped* out of my hand.
LOUISE. Well, don't be so careless again.

(SIMPSON *goes on her hands and knees to pick up pieces.* LOUISE *turns away.* SIMPSON, *while picking up the pieces—whilst on her knees—makes frantic signs to* AUBREY *who is watching—nose sign.*)

(SIMPSON, *still on her knees, insists on giving nose sign—works up towards double doors,* AUBREY *follows her up stage—when near double doors he says.*)

AUBREY. I shot a man in Mexico once for doing that!

(SIMPSON *exits hurriedly through double doors, looking amazed.*)

(AUBREY *comes down and stands by table* C.)

(*Quickly.*) Louise, what's the matter with her? She didn't drop that muffin dish for nothing. Does she suspect?
LOUISE (*comes* C.). I don't think so—why?
AUBREY (*crosses* R.). She was making the most extraordinary signs to me. (*Sits at fireplace.*)
LOUISE. Never mind that, let's finish this dying business. Somebody will be here directly.
AUBREY. Well, how am I going to die this time?
LOUISE (*slowly*). I think, darling, you'd better be drowned.

(LOUISE *gets small foot-stool and puts it down t. of* MISS MULLETT'S *chair, and sits at* AUBREY'S *feet.* AUBREY *looks amazedly at* LOUISE.)

Yes, I think drowning's the best thing for you. (*Thoughtfully.*) You see, your body must never be recovered—that's why I suggest drowning.

AUBREY. D'you propose tying a brick round my neck?

LOUISE. Oh, no, that won't be necessary. You can go down to the river to bathe.

AUBREY. It's beastly cold for bathing.

LOUISE. I can't help that. Undress in the arbour down by the cedar tree, and plunge into the river.

AUBREY. Yes, but what about a costume?

LOUISE. Go in without one!

AUBREY. It's not respectable to be drowned with nothing on

(SPRULES *comes in at that moment with another tray through double doors. He gives a cough and deliberately throws the tray on the floor up* R.C. LOUISE *springs up.*)

LOUISE. Good heavens, Sprules, what *are* you doing?

(AUBREY *jumps up, and stands behind* MISS MULLETT'S *chair, staring at* SPRULES.)

SPRULES. I'm so sorry, ma'am. But it jumped out of my hands like.

LOUISE. I don't know what's the matter with you all to-day.

(LOUISE *turns away annoyed.* SPRULES *endeavours by nose sign to catch* AUBREY'S *attention.* LOUISE *turns round.*)

Pick up that tray and go away.

(SPRULES *picks up tray, continues nose sign until off.*)

(*Exit* SPRULES *through double doors.*)

AUBREY (*comes down* C. ; *amazed*). There *is* something the matter with the servants to-day, Louise.

LOUISE. Never mind! Now, where were we?

AUBREY. I was in the river—with nothing on.

LOUISE. Oh yes! (*Up stage.*) I'll go and get another suit of yours—and I'll put it in the boathouse over there. (*Points* L.)

AUBREY. What for? (*Follows her up.*)

LOUISE. Why, that's what you've got to put on when you come out.

AUBREY (*sarcastically*). Oh, I do come out? (*Comes down.*)

(AUBREY L. ; LOUISE C.)

LOUISE. After you've gone in, I'll go down to the arbour—

(*points up stage*)—the arbour, mark you—(*points* R.)—and get the clothes you're wearing—the ones you'll take off when you go into the water—then I'll bring them back here, say I've found them in the arbour and I think something must have happened to you.

AUBREY. And you'll probably be right.

LOUISE (*triumphantly*). Then everybody will at once rush down to the *arbour* and begin searching for you.

AUBREY. I suppose I sit at the bottom like a submarine and sing "I'm for ever blowing bubbles." (*Sits on settle.*)

LOUISE. Of course not! By that time you'll have swum to the other end, fetched your clothes out of the boathouse, changed comfortably——

AUBREY. I hope so!

LOUISE. —and got away!

AUBREY. Who do I appear as next—Lilian Gish?

LOUISE. Anything—what does it matter? (*Goes down* R.) Come down as Smith or Jones or Brown, and I'll pass you off as an old friend.

AUBREY. Well, as long as you keep Giles on a chain I don't mind what I do. (*Rises, comes to* LOUISE.)

LOUISE. Right. Now clear off while they're all out of the way, and I'll——

(*Enter* MISS EVERARD *double doors. Comes down, stands between* AUBREY *and* LOUISE. LOUISE *gives a gesture of annoyance.*)

JEAN (*coyly*). Talking of me? (C.)

(LOUISE R.C.—JEAN C.— AUBREY L.C.)

LOUISE. Yes, dear, we were just wondering when you were coming down.

AUBREY. Are you feeling better, dearest? (*Taking* JEAN'S *arm.*)

JEAN. Much better, thank you, darling!

LOUISE. You're sure you're wise in coming down? (*Takes* JEAN'S *arm.*)

AUBREY. Yes, you'd better lie down again.

(*All turn up stage, but* JEAN *turns down again. They follow her arriving down stage—*AUBREY R.C.—JEAN C.—LOUISE L.C.)

JEAN. How thoughtful you are, George darling—but I'm quite all right.

LOUISE. But wouldn't you like to lie down again?

JEAN. No, I'm going to get George to take me for a little walk in the garden. (*Cross* L. *with* AUBREY, *so they are in the following positions :*

LOUISE R.C.—JEAN L.C.—AUBREY L.)

LOUISE. I don't think it would be wise, Jean.

AUBREY. These afternoons are very treacherous in the morning.
LOUISE. I should feel much happier if you were lying down.
AUBREY. So should I.
JEAN (*smiling*). How nice to have somebody who thinks about me, but I'll tell you what I will do.

(AUBREY *and* LOUISE *look at* JEAN *eagerly.*)

I'll have a chair in the garden, and I'll sit and watch the river. (*Going towards window, turns towards river.*)

AUBREY (*stopping* JEAN *up* C.) I don't think the river's running to-day.

(*Enter* MISS MULLETT *through double doors.*)

MISS MULLETT. Louise, will you tell Sprules to take a chair out in the garden for me.

(LOUISE *takes her arm.*)

LOUISE. Oh, auntie, stay with us for a little. (*Leading* MISS MULLETT *towards chair* R.) Mr. Maitland is going to—er—going to tell you some of his adventures.

(MISS MULLETT R. *of* LOUISE *who is* R.C.; JEAN *up* L.C.; AUBREY *up* L.)

(AUBREY *goes and looks rapidly over all the books in the case* L.)

JEAN. Oh, how nice! (*Coming down in front of* MISS MULLETT *and* LOUISE *to easy chair* R. *by fireplace, sits.*)

LOUISE. You wouldn't believe what he's been through, auntie.

MISS MULLETT (*going towards her chair, is very annoyed as* JEAN *is sitting there*). No, I probably shouldn't, my dear. (*Sits in other armchair down* R.)

JEAN. I always said truth is stronger than fiction.

MISS MULLETT. It's more uncommon.

(MISS MULLETT *chair* R.—JEAN *chair by fire*—LOUISE R.C.—AUBREY L. *by book-case.*)

LOUISE. Now, Cousin George,—we're ready.

AUBREY. What shall I tell you? (*Turning to* C. *up stage.*)

MISS MULLETT (*rising*). I'll go and get my spectacles.

LOUISE (*quickly stopping her*). I will, auntie. (*Going towards door.*) What sort of weather have you been having in Mexico, Mr. Maitland?

(JEAN *in chair by fireplace.* LOUISE *pushes chair by grandfather clock down stage* R.C. *for* AUBREY *to sit in to tell his adventures.*)

AUBREY. Thick and clear!

Miss Mullett (*to* Jean). Men are all alike, my dear, I don't trust any of them.

Louise (*aside to* Aubrey). Keep going, I'll slip down to the boathouse with your clothes.

Jean (*to* Miss Mullett). One wouldn't like to be without them.

Aubrey. Ah, it's an interesting little town, Mexico.

(*Exit* Louise *through double doors.*)

Miss Mullett (*to* Aubrey). Do people in Mexico go to church on Sundays, Mr. Maitland ?

Aubrey. Oh, yes, twice sometimes—twice a year. (c.)

Miss Mullett. What hymns do they use ?

Aubrey. Oh, any hymns they can get.

Miss Mullett. Ancient and Modern ?

Aubrey. Eton and Harrow. Well, on the Modern side.

Jean. Did you ever see any lions, George ?

Aubrey. Oh—hundreds prancing round on the beach there.

Jean. Oh, how thrilling !

Aubrey. I was once attacked by some. (*Putting his* R. *foot on chair and stroking his beard.*)

Jean. Were you really—how many ?

Miss Mullett (*counting her knitting*). 15—16—17—18—19——

Aubrey (*butting in*). Oh, not quite as many as that.

Jean. Oh, Miss Mullett—do listen, George was once attacked by lions—he's going to tell us all about it.

Aubrey (*dramatically*). I was *lying*—lying in bed when suddenly I awoke with a start. (*Cross* L.C.) It was as black as ink all around me, but in the open doorway—(*pointing up stage* R. *Seeing* Louise *about to cross from double doors to French windows with clothes, points down stage* L.)—No, no, that doorway ! I made out two shadowy forms.

(Louise *steals across with bundle of clothes—exit through French windows to* R.)

Miss Mullett. That's why I always keep my door shut.

Aubrey. Just at that moment, the clock struck one.

Miss Mullett. And you struck the other.

Aubrey. I sprang out of bed—snatched up a gun.

Miss Mullett (*to* Jean). Snatched up a bun !

Aubrey. Let fly with both currents—with both barrels—(*pause*)—when I struck a match, they were all three of them dead—both of them. (*Sits in chair.*)

Jean. Dead ?

Aubrey. Yes. They've been dead for years.

(*Dramatic pause.*)

Miss Mullett. What made you keep barrels of currants in your bedroom ?

JEAN. George was in the diggings you know, Miss Mullett.
MISS MULLETT. Indeed, I suppose the hotels were too expensive.
AUBREY (*very heavily*). Hotels! Woman! we've got no hotels out there. We live way up on the plains—down on the mountains—we were just a bunch of wild mice frightened to death—(*pause*)—of nothing.
MISS MULLETT. I don't wonder; I should be wild if I had to live in diggings—(*pause*)—I thought someone went for my spectacles.
JEAN. Yes, Louise did. (*Rising.* AUBREY *sits her down.*)
AUBREY (*hurriedly*). I was taken prisoner by Indians once, Miss Mullett.
MISS MULLETT (*calmly*). Why did they let you go again?
JEAN. George escaped.
MISS MULLETT. How?
AUBREY (*desperately*). Oh, I—er—swam away.
MISS MULLETT. Oh, it was an island, then?
AUBREY (*obviously uncomfortable*). Oh, yes, it was an island.
MISS MULLETT. I didn't know they had islands in Mexico.
JEAN. Do they have islands in Mexico, George?
AUBREY. Have you ever been to Mexico?
JEAN. Never.
AUBREY. Sure?
JEAN. Quite certain.
AUBREY. Then they have. Oh, yes, they've had 'em for years. Not big ones, you know—er—little ones—with water all round them.
MISS MULLETT. I should have taken a boat.
AUBREY. There weren't no boats there.
MISS MULLETT. Then how did the Indians get you across?
AUBREY (*foot on chair—reflectively*). Well, I promised I wouldn't tell. (*Sits.*)
JEAN. Why didn't you kill the Indians, George?
AUBREY. I can't think of everything. (*Rises.*)
MISS MULLETT. Where has Louise got to? (*Rising.*)
AUBREY (*quickly putting* MISS MULLETT *down again*). Sit down, kid, I've got more to tell you—I could tell you stories you'd never credit.

(LOUISE *crosses from French windows to double doors ready to come forward as if coming from upstairs.*)

MISS MULLETT. I'm sure of that.

(*Enter* LOUISE *through double doors, bangs door on entering, she carries spectacles and is obviously out of breath and flushed.*)

(*To* LOUISE.) You've been a long time, Louise.
LOUISE (*comes down behind* MISS MULLETT'S *chair*). Yes, dear, I couldn't find them. (*Handing specs. to* MISS MULLETT.)

(LOUISE *nods to* AUBREY—*meaning everything all right.*)

Miss Mullett. Why, you're out of breath.
Louise. Am I?
Jean. Obviously, dear.
Louise. I ran downstairs. (*Stands behind* Miss Mullett's *chair, in which* Jean *is sitting.*)
Miss Mullett. But my spectacles were in the dining-room.
Aubrey (*helping* Louise *out*). So you ran upstairs.
Louise. Yes, I ran upstairs and then downstairs, and—er—that's why I'm out of breath.
Miss Mullett. I see.

(*There is a slight pause,* Miss Mullett *is knitting.* Louise *makes frantic signals to* Aubrey *to go into the garden,* Aubrey *goes towards garden.*)

Louise. If you would like to have a pipe in the garden, Cousin George, don't let us stop you.
Aubrey. Think I will. (*Takes his hat from under settle, and going up to French windows.*) That river of yours looks tempting, Mrs. Allington.
Jean. You always were a great swimmer, George, weren't you?
Aubrey. Yes! Was I? (*From up stage.*)
Jean. Oh, but let me come with you, darling! (*Goes up* R. *toward* Aubrey.)
Louise (*hurriedly*). Oh, Jean, don't go for a minute. I want to talk to you. (*To* Aubrey.) You can spare her for a few minutes, can't you, Cousin George?

(Miss Mullett R. *in chair;* Louise R.C.; Jean *up* C.; Aubrey *up* L.C.)

Aubrey. Well, you're asking a lot; you know, I haven't seen her for five years, still I'll do my best. (*Kisses* Jean.) I'll see you in the river. (*Up towards French windows.*)

(*He puts on hat and exits to garden* L. *through French windows.*)

Jean (*sitting* R. *again*). Well, dear? What is it?

(Louise *goes over and closes the French windows.*)

Louise. You don't mind if I close the windows, do you? I'm feeling a little chilly.
Miss Mullett. I don't wonder. You don't wear enough clothes.
Jean. You're not feeling ill, are you, Louise? (*Rising and coming* C. *to* Louise.)
Louise. I'm not feeling very well.
Jean. Shall I get you some smelling-salts?

(Jean *goes towards French windows and looks out.* Louise *follows her and brings her down.*)

(MISS MULLETT *in chair down* R.—LOUISE C.—JEAN L.C.).

LOUISE (*clutching her*). No, no, no! I wouldn't have you go for anything.

(JEAN *goes down to settle and sits.*)

MISS MULLETT (*counting her knitting*). When I was a girl we always took smelling-salts.

LOUISE. I don't like them. They always make me sneeze.

(MISS MULLETT *rises—goes up stage* R.)

(*Quickly, as if to stop her going into the garden.*) Where are you going?

MISS MULLETT. To get some more wool, dear.

LOUISE (*eagerly*). Let me get it for you!

MISS MULLETT. No, thank you, my dear! I'll get it quicker myself.

(*Exits through double doors.*)

(LOUISE *glances anxiously out of windows.*)

JEAN. You're not worried about anything, are you, Louise?

LOUISE. Oh no, dear, not at all!

JEAN. I'm glad of that! For my part—I shall *never* forget to-day!

LOUISE. I don't think I shall either! (*Cross* R.)

JEAN (*ecstatically*). When I went upstairs with George half an hour ago—it didn't seem right with you down here!

LOUISE. It wasn't—I mean it didn't. (*Coming* C. *still with her attention on the garden.*)

JEAN. I kept on saying to myself "Can it last?"

LOUISE (*emphatically*). No! I mean yes. (*Sits beside* JEAN *on settle.*)

JEAN. You don't know how grateful I am to you, Louise! But for you this would never have happened!

(JEAN *continues to talk without noticing* LOUISE'S *annoyance and impatience.*)

The dear fellow is even more lover-like than he used to be!

LOUISE. Is he?

JEAN. What I like about George is that he's so thoughtful of others in spite of our happiness. Why he even remembered you, dear!

LOUISE. Fancy that!

JEAN. Yes, wasn't it strange? I mean, you know, really you would have been the last person one would expect him to think of!

LOUISE. Of course!

JEAN. But no! He spoke *so* nicely about you! He almost seemed worried about you!

LOUISE. You amaze me! (*With an effort.*) Ye-es! (*Looks towards window.*)

JEAN (*confidentially*). And even asked, dear, that we shouldn't kiss each other too much in front of you in case it awakened painful memories.

LOUISE. Very thoughtful of him.

JEAN. Wasn't it? But the dear fellow—(*Bus. smiling to herself*) —said we could make up for it when you weren't there.

LOUISE. Oh, he said that, did he?

JEAN. Of course you know, dear, George never dreamed I was going to tell you all this.

LOUISE. I don't suppose he did.

JEAN. George has a very reserved nature—he has hidden depths that you would never dream of.

LOUISE. I'm beginning to think so.

JEAN. He'd be frightfully upset if he thought I had told you.

LOUISE. That I can quite believe.

(*Enter* SPRULES *through double doors.*)

SPRULES. Shall I clear away tea, Madam?

LOUISE. Yes, Sprules. Do you know if Miss Mullett found her wool?

(SPRULES *moves cup and saucer from table to tray.*)

SPRULES. It was not in her room, so she's gone down to the arbour to look for it.

(LOUISE *coughs.*)

(SPRULES *exits with tray with tea things through double doors.*)

JEAN. What is it, Louise?

LOUISE. Only a frog in my throat.

JEAN. I think, darling, if you don't mind, I'll go down to the arbour too. (*Rises.*)

LOUISE. No, no, I shouldn't go.

JEAN. I'd like to watch George swim.

(*Enter* MISS MULLETT *with suit of clothes from* R. *at window—comes down* R. JEAN *crosses to her.*)

Why, Miss Mullett, what have you got there?

MISS MULLETT (R., *coming down*). I found them in the arbour; the way people leave things about is simply disgraceful.

LOUISE (L. *to* JEAN). Why, they're your husband's clothes, Jean!

JEAN (C. *to* LOUISE). All right, dear, I'll explain! (*To* MISS MULLETT :)

(LOUISE *must express delight on her face.*)

Those are my husband's clothes, Miss Mullett.

MISS MULLETT. What, my dear?

(*Enter* SPRULES *through double doors.*)

JEAN (*taking clothes*). Sprules, run down to the arbour with these clothes, quickly, they belong to Mr. Maitland. He's gone for a swim. (*Hands* SPRULES *clothes.*)

SPRULES (*with alacrity*). Yes, ma'am.

(*Goes off hurriedly through French windows with clothes.*)

MISS MULLETT. What are you doing with those clothes, my dear?
LOUISE. We're sending Sprules back to the arbour with them, auntie.
MISS MULLETT. Why?
JEAN. Because they are my husband's, Miss Mullett.
MISS MULLETT. Well, he shouldn't leave them about.
LOUISE. But he's gone for a swim, auntie.
JEAN. So when he comes out again, he'll want them.
MISS MULLETT. Oh, I see. Now, why ever didn't you tell me that before?

(SPRULES *enters hurriedly through French windows, stands on steps still with clothes.*)

SPRULES. I can see the whole of the reach of the river from the lawn, but there's no sign of Mr. Maitland anywhere. (*All turn to him.*)

(MULLETT R.—JEAN R.C.—SPRULES *at window*—LOUISE L.)

JEAN. What!
LOUISE. Jean! he can't have got cramp. He had it once when —I mean—— (*Very confused.*) Didn't I hear him say something

---

(SPRULES *comes down stage and stands behind tea-table.*)

JEAN. Good heavens! Suppose something's happened to him!

(*Rushes out through window.*)

MISS MULLETT. What's the matter now, dear?
LOUISE. Nothing, auntie, it's all right. But we're wondering whether Cousin George mightn't have got a cramp in the river and——

(SPRULES *behind tea-table.*)

MISS MULLETT. Cramp in the liver! Good heavens!

(MISS MULLETT *exits double doors.*)

SPRULES (*hesitating*). Shall—shall I go too, madam? (*Crosses to double doors.*)

LOUISE. Yes—yes—go by all means, Sprules, and take all of the servants with you! All of them, mind you. Don't stand staring there, man—do it!

(SPRULES *must convey that he thinks it is his brother.*)

SPRULES. Very good, ma'am.

(*Exit through double doors.*)

(LOUISE *crosses and falls into chair down* R.)

LOUISE. It's all right! It's all right!

(*Enter* GILES, *at French windows from* L., *carrying bundle of light clothes.*)

GILES (*comes down* L. *of* LOUISE *who is down* R.). Found them in the boathouse.

LOUISE (*rising*). You—you—found them in the boathouse?

GILES. Nice suit of clothes, too!

LOUISE. Oh, my heavens, you've ruined everything.

GILES. Anything wrong?

LOUISE. Wrong? Everything's wrong. (*Cross* L.) He's got no clothes at all now. Oh, the idiot, the imbecile. Here—(*crosses to* GILES R.C.)—give them to me! (*Snatches clothes and crosses* GILES.) And go away and leave me alone.

GILES. I'll go and see if there are any more there. (*Goes to window.*)

LOUISE. No, no! Anywhere but that. Go to the kitchen.

GILES. The kitchen? What about cook?

LOUISE. Oh, hang cook.

GILES. Very good, mum.

(*Exit double doors.*)

(LOUISE *falls helpless into chair down* R. *holding clothes. As she does so—*

AUBREY *enters through French windows from* R., *comes down* C. *He is practically naked, except for things he has found in the boathouse —carpet draped round him; with boat cushions in front and behind tied round his waist with tiller ropes. Rudder attached to his back. He is dripping with water and half his beard is hanging loose.*)

(HOLD PICTURE.)

AUBREY. This is the last time I'll ever die. (*He turns to exit through double doors, showing rudder to audience.*)

CURTAIN.

ACT III

SCENE.—*Same as last.*

TIME.—*Late afternoon of the next day.*

(*As the* CURTAIN *goes up* SPRULES *and* SIMPSON *enter from doors* R. SPRULES *crosses to settle, looking under cushions;* SIMPSON *goes down* R., *looks about mantelpiece; they are apparently searching for something.*)

SIMPSON. I can't find her blooming spectacles anywhere.

SPRULES. Oh, blow her spectacles, I expect she's sitting on them somewhere.

SIMPSON. You can say what you like, Mr. Sprules—(*crossing to* L.C. *to table by settle*)—there's a fatality haunting this house.

SPRULES. There is something unlucky about it. (*Moves across in front to* R.)

SIMPSON. Unlucky! I should say so. First the master gets exploded. Then your brother gets drowned, and now I've gone and lost my best brooch.

SPRULES. Well, let's hope that's the finish of it, anyway. (*Sits arm-chair* R.) Poor old 'Enery, fancy his being drowned; still I'm not sure that it isn't all for the best.

SIMPSON (*crossing* R.). Why, Mr. Sprules? (*Sits on arm of chair, putting her arm round* SPRULES' *shoulder.*)

SPRULES (*contemptuously*). Why, did you notice the way he was carrying on with that Miss Everard?

SIMPSON. I should think I did.

SPRULES. Another two days of that, and he'd have forgotten what he come down here for, but then 'Enery always was a fool where ladies were concerned.

SIMPSON. Fancy that! and 'im a married man too.

SPRULES. That's not his fault, it's his nature. I always said 'Enery would have made a faithful husband to any woman, providing he was married to someone else.

SIMPSON. He was on the stage, wasn't he?

SPRULES. Yes, scene shifter. (*Looking up at her.*)

SIMPSON. I thought as much—he clicked with her all right.

SPRULES. Yes, she seemed to make him clean balmy. I passed him on the stairs yesterday, as he was taking her up to her room, and I whispered "How are you going?"—then gave him the sign (*nose*)—why, he stared at me as if I was mad.

SIMPSON. His mind wasn't on his work—look at him over the muffin dish. I dented it in three places, trying to attract his attention.

SPRULES (*gloomily*). A lot of notice he took, didn't he?

SIMPSON (*rises, cross to settle* L.). What I wants to know is what's going to happen if they find his body;. they'll know in a moment then who he is. (*Sits up stage end.*)

(SPRULES *rises, going to chair* R. *of telephone table* L.C.)

SPRULES (*speaking across the table*). Let's hope they won't find it.

SIMPSON. Not now the real George Maitland himself's coming down to-day.

SPRULES. I shall never forget yesterday afternoon, as long as I live. (*Moves chair out and sits, leaning over table.*)

SIMPSON. More shall I. When she heard your brother was drowned, that Miss Everard goes off into hysterics, because she's lost her husband.

SPRULES. Then Chesterman rings up to say he was a fraud, and the real one's coming down.

SIMPSON. So she has another go of hysterics.

SPRULES. I bet her husband who's coming down to-day wouldn't half laugh if he knew how she's been carrying on with poor old 'Enery.

SIMPSON. Well, she'll never tell him.

SPRULES. Not likely.

SIMPSON. Oh, if only you'd known he was coming, Mr. Sprules, you'd have saved your brother's life!

SPRULES. Don't rub it in. (*Rises and crosses to* R., *takes handkerchief from his inside pocket and starts to cry.*) It's bad enough to think he's drowned, without remembering each time that I sort of led him into it—— (*Crying.*)

(SPRULES *down* R. SIMPSON *rises and comes up to him, tries to soothe him. Voices heard off.*)

Look out, this is probably him. (*Both busy themselves looking about the room on the* R.)

(HENERY, *disguised as* GEORGE MAITLAND, *comes in at the windows from* L. *with* LOUISE. *He is wearing navy blue suit, double-breasted, and large grey felt hat, and appears a little ill at ease, although he attempts to cover it up. During the next few lines until the exit of* SPRULES *and* SIMPSON, *he makes frantic endeavours to catch their eyes, checking himself each time* LOUISE *looks at him, and turning his gesticulations off into something else.* LOUISE *comes down* L. HENERY *stands* C.)

LOUISE. Well, Cousin George, so you've actually got here at last. Mr. Chesterman said you were coming.

(LOUISE *puts cushion straight and sits on settle.*)

HENERY (*still trying to attract* SPRULES' *attention, but failing*). He is the lawyer man, isn't he?

LOUISE. Yes, I expect him here this afternoon to meet you.

(*Catching sight of* SPRULES *and* SIMPSON *who are still busy searching under cushions, etc.*)

What are you doing, Simpson—Sprules?

SPRULES (*turning towards* LOUISE, *but not taking notice of* HENERY). Looking for Miss Mullett's spectacles.

(*Exit* SPRULES *and* SIMPSON *through double doors.*)

HENERY (*nervously—after following* SPRULES *to doors, trying to attract his attention*). Of course I am. Who did you think I was? (*Sits on chair* R. *of telephone table.*)

LOUISE (*smiling*). Oh, we've had rather curious things happening lately.

(*Enter* MISS MULLETT *through double doors.*)

MISS MULLETT. Louise, have you seen my spectacles? (*Comes down* R., *looking on mantelpiece, does not see* HENERY.)

LOUISE. No, auntie. Auntie, let me introduce you to Mr. George Maitland—my aunt, Miss Mullett. (*Sits on settle.*)

HENERY (*stands and bobs awkwardly*). How-do-you-do, Miss Mullett, how-do-you-do? Delighted to meet you, I'm sure. (*Sits.*)

MISS MULLETT (R.). I suppose you really are George Maitland?

HENERY (*startled*). Er—of course I am. Who did you think I was?

LOUISE (*smiling*). Well, we had another one here yesterday.

HENERY (*jumping up*). What?

LOUISE. I knew it would surprise you.

HENERY (*looking towards door*). W-w-where—where is he?

MISS MULLETT (*calmly*). He's drowned. (*Sits in her chair* R.)

(HENERY *gazes at* MISS MULLETT *horror-struck.*)

LOUISE. He was evidently a very clever impostor.
MISS MULLETT. I call him a blackguard.
LOUISE. Oh, auntie!
MISS MULLETT. I do, my dear, an absolute blackguard.
HENERY. Well, what do you think of that!

LOUISE. Do sit down. Of course now we've got Cousin George here it's all right.

HENERY (*sitting down, rather relieved*). Yes, of course, but it naturally surprised a chap a bit, what ?

LOUISE. He did it very cleverly, you know. He deceived us all.

MISS MULLETT. Yes, even your wife, Mr. Maitland.

HENERY (*amazed*). My—which ? (*Stands.*)

MISS MULLETT. Your wife !

(HENERY *is regarding them with horror. He looks round at doors* R. *and scratches his elbow.* MISS MULLETT *is knitting and* LOUISE *is talking quite carelessly, taking no notice of him.*)

LOUISE. Of course, you didn't know your wife was here !

HENERY. Er—er—no ! I didn't ! (*Sits.*)

MISS MULLETT. Another little surprise for you.

LOUISE. She's so sweet !

MISS MULLETT. I can't think why you've left her so long.

LOUISE. I wonder where she is. (*Cross* R. *and rings bell at fireplace, and sits in arm-chair down* R. *of* MISS MULLETT.)

HENERY (*helplessly*). What's she like ? Is she like what she was like—I mean—has she altered much ?

LOUISE. No, I don't think so—why ?

HENERY (*eagerly*). *I* have, you know—an awful lot. (*Stands.*)

MISS MULLETT. Surely you could have found time to write to her, Mr. Maitland ?

HENERY. I can't write—I can't write much in Mexico. (*Floundering for words.*)

(*Enter* SPRULES *through double doors—*HENERY *vainly endeavours by means of signs to attract his attention.*)

LOUISE. Sprules, where is Miss Everard ?

SPRULES. In the garden, ma'am. (*Down* R.C.—*keeping his eyes on* LOUISE.)

LOUISE. Tell her that Mr. Maitland is here.

SPRULES. Yes, ma'am.

(*As he goes towards exit he pretends to pick up a bit of fluff from the carpet.* HENERY *tries to touch him with his hat.* SPRULES *exits into garden and off* L.)

HENERY (*making excuses to get out after* SPRULES). Shall I go and find her ?

LOUISE. Oh, no ! Do sit down ! Sprules will tell her.

HENERY (*coming down* C.). You know, I expect I'm awfully changed since she last saw me.

LOUISE. So you were saying.

MISS MULLETT. Love can penetrate any disguise.

HENERY. That's what I was thinking. (*Going slightly* L.)

Miss Mullett. When I was a girl I always used to say these unexpected surprises were the nicest.

(*Enter* Jean *from garden. She crosses down* R.C., *does not see* Henery.)

Louise. Ah, here she is! (*Rises to meet* Jean R.C.)

(Henery, *who is* L. *in front of settle, gazes at her.*)

Jean (*not believing her eyes*). George—George—is it really you?

(Miss Mullett *in her chair* R.—Louise R.C.—Jean C.—Henery L.)

Henery (*nervously*). Y-y-yes, d-d-darling. It's m-m-me all right.

Jean (*going* L. *to* Henery). Oh, George! (*Falls into his arms—embrace.*)

(*They both sit on settle—*Jean *down stage end*—Louise *goes to* Miss Mullett's L.)

It is really you, George, isn't it? (*Taking his arm.*)
Henery. Oh yes, darling, it's nobody else.
Jean (*gazing at* Henery). Yes, I'm sure it is.
Henery. I'm certain of it too.
Jean. George, you can kiss me.

(Henery *looks nervously at* Miss Mullett *and* Louise.)

Miss Mullett. You needn't mind us.

(Jean *and* Henery *kiss.* Louise *sits on small footstool* L. *of* Miss Mullett.)

Jean (*sighing*). I could have told you anywhere, George, by the way you kiss. (*She sits close to* Henery.) You've been away such a long time, darling.
Miss Mullett. I understood you were shot, Mr. Maitland.
Henery (*startled*). Shot!
Jean. Yes, darling, in Mexico.
Miss Mullett. In a saloon.
Jean. Where were you wounded, George?
Henery. In the saloon—I forgot.
Louise. Forgot, Cousin George! How could you!
Jean. When your friend wrote and said you risked your life for another.
Henery (*bravely*). Oh, it's nothing. We do that every day in Nevada.
Jean. Nevada—I never knew you were in Nevada. (*Surprised.*)
Henery. Yes; I went there for a week-end. (*Getting very muddled.*)
Miss Mullett. So you weren't shot, Mr. Maitland?

HENERY. Oh, yes, I was shot all right, but it wasn't really serious, you know. (*Pulling himself together.*)

JEAN. But if it wasn't serious, George, why have you never written?

HENERY (*confused*). Well, my dear—er—er—I hadn't got a stamp.

JEAN (*tearfully*). You've been away so long, George.

HENERY. Oh, ten years is nothing in Mexico.

JEAN. Ten! It's not five since you left England.

HENERY (*sentimentally*). It's seemed like ten, darling.

(*Pause.* HENERY *is obviously nervous.*)

I've—I've had some extraordinary adventures since I left England.

MISS MULLETT (*quickly*). Tell us some.

HENERY. Oh, it would take too long. (*Standing.*)

JEAN. Oh, do, George! (*Pulling* HENERY *down on settle again.*)

LOUISE. We should simply love to hear them.

MISS MULLETT. Ever taken prisoner by Indians?

HENERY. Er—no!

MISS MULLETT. The other George Maitland was.

LOUISE. But he was an impostor, auntie.

MISS MULLETT. All men are!

JEAN. Not *all* men, Miss Mullett. (*Putting arm round* GEORGE'S *neck.*)

MISS MULLETT. My dear mother used to say "Show me a man and I'll show you the Devil!"

JEAN. George darling, d'you remember the pet name you always used to call me? (*Nestling up to* HENERY.)

HENERY. Do I remember it? As if I could ever forget! Er—let me see now—what was it again?

JEAN (*coyly*). Little Blossom!

MISS MULLETT. What! Little opossum?

LOUISE. Blossom, auntie!

MISS MULLETT. When I was a girl I was called Cupid.

HENERY. I know. That little bloke with nothing on what says: "Thumbs up!"

(MISS MULLETT *stares at him indignantly. Enter* SPRULES *through double doors, stands* R. *of them.*)

SPRULES. Mr. Chesterman to see you, ma'am.

(LOUISE *rises and comes* C. *Enter* CHESTERMAN *through double doors.*)

(*Exit* SPRULES *through double doors.*)

CHESTERMAN. Ah, how-do-you-do, Mrs. Allington? (*Shakes hands.*)

(Miss Mullett r.—Chesterman r.c.—Louise c.—Henery l.c.—
  Jean l.)

Louise. How are you, Mr. Chesterman? You know everyone, I think?

(Chesterman *bows all round, then stares at* Henery.)

Oh, this is Mr. George Maitland.

(Chesterman *crosses in front of* Louise *to* Henery *and shakes hands.*)

Chesterman. This is the George Maitland at last, I hope?

Henery (*rising, nettled*). Wot's the game? Everyone's asked me that.

Chesterman. Well, you can hardly wonder, Mr. Maitland. We've had an impostor here yesterday.

(Miss Mullett *seated* r.—Louise r.c.—Chesterman c.—Henery *top of settle, standing*—Jean l. *on settle.*)

Henery. Yes, so I've 'eard—(*coughs*)—heard!

Miss Mullett. I call him a blackguard.

Louise. Oh, auntie!

Chesterman. That's really what I came down for, Mrs. Allington.

Louise. Oh, a dreadful thing happened—he's drowned.

Chesterman (*amazed*). Drowned!!!

Jean. Yes, he went down to the river to bathe——

Henery. Like Adam and Eve and pinch me——

(*All shocked.*)

Jean. We found his clothes, but his body has never been recovered.

Chesterman. What an amazing thing!

Henery (*jocularly*). P'raps he heard I'd turned up—and got nervous.

Jean. That's what *I* believe.

Chesterman. I wonder who he was.

Louise. I can't think!

Miss Mullett. Well, the body's sure to be recovered, and then we shall know.

Chesterman. When did you arrive in England, Mr. Maitland?

Henery. Er—last—yesterday.

Jean. Oh, if only you'd come down then, George!

Chesterman (*laughing*). It would have been funny, wouldn't it?

Louise. It would, indeed! (*Crosses to* r. *corner behind* Miss Mullett *and sits in chair on her* r.)

Henery. You got my telegram all right, Mr. Cheeseman.

Jean. Chesterman, dear.

CHESTERMAN. Yes, thank you, Mr. Maitland, but why did you send two?

HENERY. I didn't.

(CHESTERMAN C.; LOUISE *extreme* R.; MISS MULLETT R.; JEAN *and* HENERY *on settle.*)

CHESTERMAN. Oh, but you did—I had them within an hour of each other.

(*Pause—during which they all look at* HENERY.)

JEAN. Why did you send two, George?

(CHESTERMAN *produces telegrams from his pocket.*)

CHESTERMAN. Here they are! One handed in at Piccadilly; (*reading*) "Just arrived in England. Going to Marlow to-morrow. Maitland." The other was handed in at Liverpool: "Just arrived in England, expect me to-morrow."

(CHESTERMAN *goes behind* MISS MULLETT *to* LOUISE *and shows her the telegrams.*)

JEAN. Why did you send two, George?

HENERY (*blankly, resuming his seat by* JEAN *on settle*). I—er—— (*Mops his face with his handkerchief.*) You know—er—I must have forgot all about it. I'm terribly absent-minded. (*Thought suddenly occurs to him.*) I lost my memory once in Mexico.

MISS MULLETT (*to* LOUISE). What did he lose, dear?

LOUISE. His memory, auntie.

MISS MULLETT. Oh, I thought it might have been something valuable.

HENERY. It was a horrible experience, Mrs. Muffett.

MISS MULLETT. (*Very annoyed.*) What was?

HENERY. The time I lost my memory.

MISS MULLETT. (*Tersely.*) What was it?

(CHESTERMAN *remains behind* MISS MULLETT'S *chair.*)

HENERY (*hurriedly*). It's too long to tell you now—but I lost it for days and days and days—and—er—days!

JEAN. How terrible for you, George!

MISS MULLETT. How did you find it again?

HENERY Oh, it—er—sort of came back—quite suddenly. I often do it now, you know. It simply goes—and when I come to myself, it's gone and I don't remember anything about it.

MISS MULLETT. Nothing at all!

HENERY. No, absolutely nothing.

Miss MULLETT (*calmly*). Then, how do you know you've ever lost it ?

(HENERY *regards* JEAN *helplessly for a moment.*)

JEAN. Why, obviously, Miss Mullett, someone tells him of the extraordinary things he has done.

HENERY (*quickly*). That's it! That's it! And then, you see, I just jump to the conclusion at once.

MISS MULLETT. Decidedly interesting!

HENERY (*feeling more at ease*). I've told you this just in case, I don't say I shall, you know—but just in case I should say or do extraordinary things here.

MISS MULLETT. You probably will. The other one did.

JEAN. But if you did, darling, is there no way to bring you round ?

LOUISE. We certainly ought to know.

HENERY. Well, you mustn't worry me at all with questions, that's the worst thing you can do. Just soothe me and—er—humour me—

(JEAN *strokes his hair.*)

—and if it gets very bad *just leave me alone.*

(*Takes* JEAN'S *hand off his head.*)

JEAN. And let you sleep it off ?

HENERY. That's it, that's it. Let me sleep it off.

JEAN. I'm glad you've told us, dear, we won't forget. (*Holding his hand.*)

LOUISE. Soothe you and humour you, and let you sleep it off.

HENERY (*emphatically*). And, of course, never refer to it again. (*Rise.*)

(*Enter* SPRULES *through double doors, comes* C.)

SPRULES (*to* LOUISE). The Reverend Ebenezer Brown to see you, ma'am.

LOUISE (*jumping up and going* C.). Mr. Brown—Mr. Brown.

SPRULES. A clergyman, madam.

LOUISE. Show him in, Sprules.

(*Exit* SPRULES *through double doors.*)

MISS MULLETT. When I was a girl I always loved clergymen.

(*Enter* SPRULES *double doors, announcing :*)

SPRULES. The Reverend Ebenezer Brown. (*Stands* R. *of door and exits after* AUBREY'S *entrance.*)

(*Enter* AUBREY. *He is disguised as a clergyman—he has red hair and wears horn-rimmed spectacles —walks on his toes and speaks in very flowery language.*)

AUBREY. Ah, my dear Mrs. Allington, this is indeed a pleasure—I suppose I can take the privilege of an old friend—— (*Shakes hands and kisses* LOUISE.)

(CHESTERMAN R. *of* MISS MULLETT; MISS MULLETT R.; AUBREY *and* LOUISE C.; HENERY L.C.; JEAN *on settle*.)

LOUISE. Oh, my dear Ebenezer, how do you do—I haven't seen you for years.
AUBREY. And you haven't been to church either, you naughty girl!
LOUISE. Let me introduce you, Mr. Ebenezer Brown—Miss Mullett, Miss Everard, Mr. Chesterman. (*Pauses and turns to* HENERY.) And this, Aubrey—Ebenezer—(*speaks nervously*)—is Mr. George Maitland, who . . .
AUBREY (*in his natural voice*). What! (*Assuming his other voice quickly*.) Pardon me, a slight twinge of my old enemy, the gout. (*Crosses to* HENERY.) Mr. George Maitland, you say. And what the hel—who may you be—doing here ?—*What* may you be doing here ?
LOUISE (*deliberately*). Mr. Maitland, Ebenezer, has only just turned up most unexpectedly from Mexico.
HENERY. Why yes, owing to Aubrey Allington's death . . .
AUBREY. A most lamentable occurrence. (*Fidgeting with his hat*.)
JEAN. You knew him, Mr. Brown ?
AUBREY. Oh, most intimately. He and I were stewed—er—students together.
HENERY. He was a top-hole chap, I've heard. (*Goes up to window*.)
AUBREY. A noble soul, Mr. Maitland. Too good for this wicked world.
LOUISE (*tearfully*). Everybody loved him.
AUBREY. How could they help it ? Ah me! here to-morrow and gone this afternoon.

(HENERY *at window*; CHESTERMAN R.; MISS MULLETT R. *in chair*; AUBREY *and* LOUISE C.; JEAN *on settle*.)

JEAN. You would scarcely credit it, Mr. Brown, but we have had an impostor down here trying to palm himself off as George Maitland.
AUBREY. Dear! Dear! You fill me with *incredulity*.
MISS MULLETT. A scoundrel of a fellow.
JEAN. Something warned me he was an impostor directly I saw him.
AUBREY. How utterly wonderful is woman's instinct.

HENERY (*chuckling*). Them's my sentiments! (*Moving down L. behind settle.*)
AUBREY. Where is this fellow now?
CHESTERMAN. He was drowned yesterday.
AUBREY (*cross to* MISS MULLETT). Dear, enough to give him his death of cold. Have you—have you any idea as to who he was?
LOUISE. Not the remotest.
AUBREY (*relieved, relaxes into his natural voice*). That's all right—(*pulling himself up*)—I mean, it *will* be all right when they find the body.
CHESTERMAN. They're bound to find it. (*Down stage* R.)
AUBREY. Of course they'll find it, Mr. Chesterman. Of course they will find it! We can't have bodies lying about in rivers. It is not healthy. (*Looking at* MISS MULLETT.) Answer me, now, would it be healthy? No—that's all right. That's all I want to know. (*Turns up stage.*)
CHESTERMAN (*to* LOUISE). Did he go out intending to bathe, Mrs. Allington?
LOUISE. Not as far as we know.
JEAN. It seems that the idea must have suddenly struck him. He apparently just took off his clothes and went in.
AUBREY. And forgot to come out, I suppose? (*Coming down* C.)
MISS MULLETT. When I was a girl we always wore costumes.
AUBREY (*very earnestly, looking at* MISS MULLETT). I hope so. (*Turns up and sits on chair in front of grandfather clock.*)
JEAN. Well, let's forget all about it. We've got you now, George.
HENERY (*smiling*). Yes, you have. (*Sitting on settle with* JEAN.)

(CHESTERMAN R.—MULLETT *in chair* R.—LOUISE R.C.—AUBREY C.—JEAN *and* HENERY *on settle.*)

CHESTERMAN (*smiling*). I hope so.
AUBREY. Indeed, something to be thankful for.

(MISS MULLETT *rises.*)

LOUISE. Where are you going, auntie?

(MISS MULLETT *goes towards window.*)

MISS MULLETT. I'm going to take my usual constitutional before dinner.
CHESTERMAN (*going up stage to* L. *of* MISS MULLETT). May I escort you, Miss Mullett?
MISS MULLETT. Oh, thank you, Mr. Chesterman.

(MISS MULLETT *and* CHESTERMAN *stand for a minute on the terrace—then exeunt to* R.)

(LOUISE *watches* MISS MULLETT—AUBREY *goes down* R., *sits.*)

JEAN (*rising and coming* c.). George dear, would you like to take me for a little stroll?

(HENERY *does not move.*)

(*Louder.*) George —— (*Looking at* HENERY.)

(HENERY *and* AUBREY *both spring to their feet.* AUBREY *realizing his mistake turns it off with a movement and sits again.* JEAN *and* HENERY *go to French windows.*)

(*Exit* JEAN *and* HENERY *into the garden to* L.)

AUBREY (*jumping up*). Louise, what on earth does this mean?
LOUISE. It's Cousin George Maitland turned up unexpectedly. (*Coming down* c.)
AUBREY. I know! I can see that! (*Pushes spectacles on top of his head.*)
LOUISE (L.). He wasn't dead.
AUBREY (R.). Why not?
LOUISE. It's not my fault, Aubrey, I can't kill everybody.
AUBREY. When did he turn up?
LOUISE. Five minutes after you left yesterday, Chesterman rang up about it, and Maitland himself came along to-day.
AUBREY. It's positively disgusting.
LOUISE. Just when we'd got everything fixed, too.
AUBREY. And now he is going to get all our money.
LOUISE. I suppose so!
AUBREY. Oh, there must be some way out.
LOUISE (*reflectively*). It's no use you dying again, is it?
AUBREY. Of course it isn't. There's only one man to die and that's George Maitland. You could try doing the cooking for a bit. If that didn't kill him nothing would. (*Chuckling.*)
LOUISE. Oh, if you're going to be rude . . . (*Cross* L. *settle and sits.*)
AUBREY. Can't you stand a joke? I must have some sort of recreation.

(*Pause.*)

LOUISE. Aubrey, *I've got an idea.*
AUBREY. Well, if you're thinking of killing me again you can keep it.
LOUISE. I'm not. Listen! why can't we square him?
AUBREY. Square him? (*Goes to* LOUISE *at settle, sits and puts his arm round her.*)
LOUISE. Yes, tell him who you are!
AUBREY. What's the good of that?
LOUISE. Why, we could threaten him with it. He's either got to share the money with us, or else you'll come to life again.
AUBREY. What a wife you'd have made for an undertaker.

LOUISE. Well, d'you think it's good?
AUBREY. Good? My dear, it's wonderful.
LOUISE. All right, now go and get George Maitland in and we'll present our ultimatum.
AUBREY. Remember, darling, you've got to be very upset and cry a lot.
LOUISE. Yes, I know.
AUBREY. Fine! We'll try and persuade him first, and if that fails, we'll threaten him.

(*Bus. of leg slipping on rug—rises—goes towards window.*)

I wonder where the old bounder is.

(AUBREY *goes to window and as he reaches it* HENERY *comes in from the window from* L.)

AUBREY (R. *of window*). Oh, here you are, Mr. Maitland. I was just looking for you.

(*The moment she hears this* LOUISE *produces a handkerchief and begins sobbing loudly.* HENERY *looks from one to the other.*)

HENERY. What's all this about? (C.)
AUBREY (R.C.). She's rather upset about something.
LOUISE (*weeping*). Oh, I don't know how to tell you, Cousin George, but I've got a confession to make.
HENERY. Well, cough it up!

(AUBREY R.; HENERY C.; LOUISE *on settle.*)

AUBREY (R.). The truth is, Mr. Maitland, that there is—er—somebody—somebody masquerading in this house—as somebody else.

(HENERY *turns in alarm.*)

(*Distinct agitation of* HENERY *imagining that* AUBREY *means him.*)

LOUISE (*tearfully*). We thought you would be surprised.
AUBREY (*gravely*). It is a bit of a shock, isn't it?

(HENERY *suddenly makes for the window, but* AUBREY *catches him by the arm.*)

No, no, no! Don't go, Mr. Maitland. We want to avoid a scandal, if possible.
HENERY (*suddenly*). Well, what are you going to do about it?
AUBREY. Well, rather, Mr. Maitland—well, rather—what are *you* going to do about it? (*Jerking his head forward into* HENERY'S *face.*)

(HENERY *dodges back.*)

HENERY. Can't it be hushed up?

LOUISE (*eagerly*). That's what I said. (*Imploringly.*) Oh Cousin George, *do* let's hush it up.

HENERY. Well, I don't want to write home about it. It's no fault of mine it ever happened.

AUBREY. My dear fellow, we shouldn't blame you. It was *the wife's* idea. (*Sits, small stool* R.C.)

HENERY (*puzzled*). The wife?

LOUISE. Yes; you see, Aubrey and I were frightfully hard up and we knew that directly we came into the money we should have our creditors all over us, so we decided that Aubrey—(*pointing to him*)—had better die. . . .

HENERY. So *you're* Aubrey Allington?

AUBREY. That's right.

HENERY. And you're the chap in the house who's masquerading!

LOUISE. Exactly!

HENERY. Well, of course that does alter things. (*His attitude immediately changes.*) Entirely. (*Deliberately.*) Well—Mr. Ebenezer Brown—Allington—what about it?

LOUISE. You see, Cousin George, thinking you were dead, Aubrey turned up as you yesterday.

HENERY. No wonder they can't find your body! (*Sitting chair by table* L.C.)

LOUISE (*smiling*). You see, we never knew you had a wife.

HENERY. No—more did I.

(*All look at each other.*)

AUBREY. What!

HENERY. I say—no more did I know that you didn't know How should I?

LOUISE. So when Aubrey turned up as you and found he was married, of course he had to die again. (*Getting up.*)

AUBREY. Then just as we were all lamenting my death you turned up and spoilt it all. (*Rising with disgust.*)

HENERY (*chuckling*). I've spoilt it all. Well, I like that!

LOUISE. You get that six thousand a year now.

HENERY. Naturally. He's dead. (*Pointing to* AUBREY.)

LOUISE. So we thought perhaps we might—er—come to some little arrangement. (*Going round settle to slightly behind* HENERY.)

HENERY. In other words—that you might touch for a bit.

AUBREY. Well, we might go halves.

LOUISE (*coming forward* C.). Aubrey's not likely to live long, you know.

AUBREY (*crossing* LOUISE). Anyone can see that. (*Looking closely into* HENERY'S *face.*)

HENERY (*sarcastically*). I suppose you wouldn't like me to give it *all* up? (*Rises. Crosses* L.)

LOUISE. Oh, no! (R.C.)

HENERY. Thank you so much.
AUBREY (C.). We shouldn't expect that.
HENERY. Well, of all the cast-iron impudence I've ever struck I think this wins it. (*Coming towards* C.)
LOUISE. Oh—Cousin George! Don't say that.
HENERY. I do say it!
AUBREY. Well, don't say it again. (*Gets* R.)
HENERY. Here am I—come all the way from Mexus-Texico at—endless trouble and expense.
LOUISE (C.). Oh, but we realize that!
HENERY. How thoughtful of you! (*Turn* L.)
LOUISE. Of course, Cousin George, you know best, but it would be a pity for Aubrey to have to come to life again . . . because if he did the money would be his entirely.
HENERY (*turning round*). Eh?
AUBREY. If I were alive, I'm the rightful heir.
LOUISE (*to* AUBREY). Still, Aubrey, if it becomes necessary to right a wrong . . .

(AUBREY R.—LOUISE C.—HENERY L.)

AUBREY (*dramatically*). Yes, whatever the cost, I can stifle my conscience no longer.

(*He and* LOUISE *strike dramatic attitude.*)

HENERY (*realizing his position*). Look here—if I agree to pay you money as long as you live, will you stay dead? Is it a bet?
AUBREY. Of course it is! (*Cross* C.)

(AUBREY *and* HENERY *shake hands.*)

HENERY. Oh, by the way, you couldn't let me nave a bit to go on with, could you? Just till old Chesterman brasses up.

(LOUISE R.C.—AUBREY C.—HENERY L.C.)

AUBREY. Certainly. How much?
HENERY. Oh, fifty or a hundred, or a couple of hundred.
AUBREY. Oh, yes; I can let you have a couple of hundred, or a hundred, or fifty. (*Taking money from wallet.*) Here's twenty-five.
HENERY (*takes money and puts it in his pocket*). I say, it's really rather funny.
AUBREY. Yes, isn't it?

(AUBREY *and* HENERY *laugh.*)

HENERY (*digging him in the ribs*). You being the Reverend Ebenezer Brown. . . .
AUBREY (*digging*). Yes, when I'm not. And you being George Maitland. . . .
HENERY (*half aside*). Yes, when I'm not—when I am, I mean.

(*Both roar with laughter.*)

LOUISE. Cousin George, you won't tell your wife about this, will you?

HENERY. Not a word! (*Laughs.*)

AUBREY. Do you know, she said to me, yesterday, "I could have told you anywhere, George, by the way you kiss."

(*Both scream with laughter. They all explode with laughter.* LOUISE *sitting in* MISS MULLETT'S *chair ;* AUBREY *in chair* R. *of* L.C. *table ;* HENERY L. *on settle. Enter* CHESTERMAN *unseen by them from garden, comes down back of settle to* L.)

CHESTERMAN. Mayn't I hear it!

(*All turn to him and become grave quickly.*)

HENERY. We were laughing at something Mr. Brown was telling us. (*Jocularly.*)

CHESTERMAN (*slyly*). I'm beginning to think Mr. Brown isn't what he appears to be.

HENERY (*laughing*). I've been thinking that for some time.

(LOUISE *in chair* R.—AUBREY *by table* L.C.—HENERY *on settle*— CHESTERMAN L.)

LOUISE (*laughing*). I'm quite sure of it.

AUBREY (*laughing*). I think you're a lot of dirty dogs—(*checks himself hastily*)—as my organist would say.

(*Enter* SIMPSON *double doors.*)

SIMPSON (*to* LOUISE). Could I speak to you for a moment, please, madam?

LOUISE (*rising and going up to her*). Yes, Simpson. (*To others.*) Please excuse me!

(LOUISE *exits with* SIMPSON *through double doors.*)

CHESTERMAN. You know, I'm rather worried about that fellow who called himself George Maitland who was drowned yesterday.

AUBREY (*still at* R. *of telephone table*). I'm not at all comfortable about him myself.

HENERY (*on settle, winking at* AUBREY). I wonder if he'll turn up again?

AUBREY (*quickly*). Oh, I shouldn't think so. (*Hits* HENERY *on chest with hat.*)

CHESTERMAN. I can't think what his motive was.

HENERY (*enjoying the joke*). I suppose he was after my money.

AUBREY (*crosses down* L. *to* CHESTERMAN, *stepping broadly over* HENERY'S *feet as he does so*). Strange is it not, this greed of gold! (*Aloud to* CHESTERMAN—*hands him case.*) Will you grasp a gasper!

CHESTERMAN. Thanks. (*Takes cigarette.*) You are sure Mrs. Allington doesn't mind smoking in here ?

(HENERY *rises to* AUBREY'S R. *hand, and takes one without being asked.*)

AUBREY (*carelessly*). Oh lord, no ! I've smoked in here ever since I married her. . . . (*Hastily.*) Since I married her to poor Aubrey.

(HENERY C.—AUBREY L.C.—CHESTERMAN L.)

CHESTERMAN. Exactly !

(AUBREY *tries to strike match on the seat of his trousers. Remembering, he pulls himself together and strikes it on box. Re-enter* LOUISE *from double doors.*)

LOUISE. Am I interrupting ? (*Takes cigarette box from sideboard, comes* C. *and hands it to* AUBREY. HENERY *gets a little* R.)

AUBREY. No, thank you. I've got one. I'll fill my case later. We were just discussing that poor soul who was drowned yesterday. (*Puts box on table* L.C.)

HENERY. We were wondering who he could be.

LOUISE. I wonder. (*She crosses* AUBREY *to settle.*)

AUBREY. I wonder ! (*Turning to her.*)

HENERY. And where he's got to !

LOUISE. I really wonder ! (*Sits up stage end of settle.*)

AUBREY. I wonder really ! (*Sitting beside her.*)

HENERY (*to* CHESTERMAN). I suppose he was really very much like me.

CHESTERMAN. He could have passed for you anywhere.

AUBREY. Oh, without a doubt.

LOUISE (*to* AUBREY). Ebenezer, you forget you never saw him.

AUBREY (*hastily*). With a doubt.

HENERY. Well, I don't suppose we shall ever see him again.

LOUISE. I, for one, hope not.

HENERY. I can quite understand that. Well, if you don't mind, I think I'll go out and join my wife. (*Turns up towards double doors.*)

(LOUISE *and* AUBREY *on settle—*CHESTERMAN *approaches them and they face* L. *to talk to him.*)

LOUISE (*without looking round at him*). Certainly, Mr. Maitland, you'll find her in the garden.

HENERY. In the garden.

(HENERY *changes direction and exits through the French windows* L.)

(*Almost as he does so, the real* GEORGE MAITLAND *appears at double doors* R., *comes down* C. *and takes position occupied by* HENERY.

The others do not see him, and continue their conversation. He is an exact double of HENERY, *dressed just like him except he wears a single-breasted blue suit and does not wear or carry a hat. He stands looking at them a little puzzled and apparently trying to speak.*)

CHESTERMAN. Well, thank goodness we've found the real George Maitland at last!

(LOUISE *and* AUBREY *are seated on settle.* CHESTERMAN L.)

LOUISE. Yes, there can be no more complications now.
MAITLAND. Pardon me . . . (C.)

(*All turn. They immediately mistake him for* HENERY. AUBREY *and* LOUISE *on settle.* CHESTERMAN *on their* L, MAITLAND C.)

LOUISE. I thought you'd gone!
MAITLAND. Gone! I've just come, I want to see Mrs. Allington.
AUBREY. As my nephews say—we'll buy it.
MAITLAND. I'm afraid I don't understand you. I'm George Maitland. . . .
AUBREY. Yes, yes, of course, we know all about that. But what is the game? (*Jumps forward and back—sits again.*)
MAITLAND. Game! There's no game. I'm George Maitland of Mexico. . . .
CHESTERMAN. Don't keep harping on it, my dear fellow. We know that.
LOUISE. Your wife's in the garden. I just told you.
MAITLAND. My wife! (*Laughs in ridicule, and goes up stage.*)

(*Picture :* CHESTERMAN, AUBREY *and* LOUISE *all look at each other in amazement.* AUBREY *and* LOUISE *rise.*)

LOUISE (*to* CHESTERMAN). Don't you see? He's lost his memory again.
CHESTERMAN. Of course. It never occurred to me.
AUBREY. How truly sad.
MAITLAND (*coming down* R.). I couldn't get any sense out of your butler, so I just walked right in.
LOUISE. Yes, yes! (*Aside to others.*) Humour him!
CHESTERMAN. ⎫
AUBREY. ⎬ Yes, yes!
MAITLAND. I'm George Maitland from Mexico. . . .

(MAITLAND R.; LOUISE R.C.; AUBREY L.C.; CHESTERMAN L.)

CHESTERMAN. ⎫
AUBREY. ⎬ Yes, yes!
LOUISE. ⎭

MAITLAND. And I've just come down to see a Mr. Chesterman....
CHESTERMAN.
AUBREY. } Yes, yes!
LOUISE.
LOUISE (*aside*). Keep it up!
MAITLAND. I sent him a wire yesterday....
CHESTERMAN.
AUBREY. } Yes, yes!
LOUISE.
MAITLAND. Don't keep saying "Yes, yes!"
AUBREY. No, no!
MAITLAND (*angrily*). Have you all gone crazy?
AUBREY. Yes, yes!
CHESTERMAN. No, no!
MAITLAND. Well, you've got me beat! (*Turns* R. LOUISE *follows him.*)
AUBREY. Sad! Sad! Sad!
LOUISE (*aloud, advancing to* MAITLAND). You know me, Mr. Maitland, don't you?
MAITLAND. Madam, I do not!
AUBREY (*to* CHESTERMAN). Oh, truly sad!
MAITLAND (*angrily*). Say, what's this stuff you're handing me? (*Cross* L.C.)
AUBREY (*moving away quickly and dodging behind and to* L. *side of* CHESTERMAN). Oh, nothing, nothing.
LOUISE (*leading* MAITLAND *round to* R. *again*). I'm Louise, George. Louise Allington—poor dear Aubrey's wife.
MAITLAND. Oh, you're Louise Allington, are you? (*Takes her hands.*)
CHESTERMAN (*to* AUBREY). He's coming to!
LOUISE (*taking one of* MAITLAND's *hands and starting to pat it*). How are you, Cousin George?
MAITLAND. Well, I shall be all right as soon as I can get anyone to talk sense.
AUBREY. Yes, yes!
MAITLAND (*getting rattled and turning on* AUBREY). Cut that out!

(AUBREY *throws his hat to* L. *corner, picks it up and then throws it across to chair which is in front of grandfather clock, and the hat-throwing being an excuse for him to get out of* MAITLAND'S *way, sits on chair in front of grandfather clock.*)

LOUISE. Now, Cousin George, come and sit down. (*Holding his hands, leading him to chair* R.)

(AUBREY *comes down, stands behind telephone table.*)

MAITLAND. I don't want to sit down. What the deuce are you doing to my hands? (*He snatches them away.*)

(*At that moment enter* JEAN *from garden through French window she also imagines him to be* HENERY. *He expresses in his face his amazement at seeing her.*)

Jean!!

(LOUISE *crosses at back of arm-chair to* C.)

JEAN (*calmly*). Well, dear, what's the matter ?

(MAITLAND R.—LOUISE *up* C.—JEAN *down* C.—AUBREY L.C.—CHESTERMAN L.)

LOUISE (*to* JEAN, *aside*). Memory's gone. Humour him!
MAITLAND. Aren't you pleased to see me?
JEAN (*aside*). The poor dear! Yes, George darling. (*Crosses to him.*) Of course I'm delighted to see you! (*Puts her arm round him.*) There, there!
AUBREY. } There, there!
CHESTERMAN. }

(AUBREY, *as he speaks, retreats to sideboard* R.)

MAITLAND (*to* JEAN). What on earth are you doing here?
JEAN (*smiles*). Well—I—er—I've just come here to be with you.
MAITLAND. What! You knew I was coming?
JEAN. Well, not exactly—but—er—why worry about it? Here we are.

(AUBREY *up at sideboard, helps himself to cigarettes, he then takes flowers out of vase and drinks the water.* MAITLAND *falls into chair* R. *helplessly.*)

MAITLAND. This gets my head buzzing like a saw-mill.
JEAN (*soothingly*). Yes, of course.
LOUISE. He is bad this time.
AUBREY. The strain's been too much. (*Comes down* R. *of* CHESTERMAN.)
MAITLAND (*savagely to* AUBREY). What d'you mean?
AUBREY (*very frightened*). No offence.

(*Pushes his hat on* CHESTERMAN'S *head, turns up stage, looks round for a way out, he opens the door of the clock, closes it, and goes through French windows to* R.)

MAITLAND. Get these guys to fade away, Jean. I don't like 'em. (*Sits in* MISS MULLETT'S *arm-chair* R.)
JEAN. Yes, dear, of course I will. (*To* CHESTERMAN *and* LOUISE.) Just leave him to me. I'll soon bring him round.

LOUISE. Don't forget—you must get him to sleep. (*Up stage, to* JEAN.)
JEAN. All right!

(LOUISE *and* CHESTERMAN *exit to* L. *French windows.*)

(AUBREY *appears at window* R. *and looks in nervously, then taps china flower-bowl to attract* JEAN'S *attention.*)

AUBREY (*to* JEAN). Give him an aspirin.

(*Exit* AUBREY *into garden to* L. *through French windows.*)

(JEAN *goes over and stands by* MAITLAND.)

MAITLAND. Now, Jean, for the love of Mike, put me wise, what's the dope they are trying to hand me?
JEAN. Oh, it's nothing, dear. It's only their little way. (*Gets behind his chair and starts massage movement over his head.*)
MAITLAND. Little way, indeed! The place is like a madhouse!
JEAN. Yes, dear, I know. (*Continuing massage business.*)
MAITLAND. What are you messing about with my head for?
JEAN. It's all right, darling. It's all right!
MAITLAND. It isn't all right. Even the butler's dippy. When I came in at the front door and asked if anyone was in he just laughed in my face.
JEAN (*soothingly*). So what did you do? (*Sits facing him on the other chair down* R.)
MAITLAND. Do? I gave him my name and told him to announce me.
JEAN (*humouring him*). And did he?
MAITLAND. No, he did not. He stared at me for a moment and then said: "You'd better 'op it quick, the real one's here."
JEAN. What a thing to say!
MAITLAND. Here am I, travelling all night, absolutely all in. . . .
JEAN. You want a good rest, darling. (*Goes to fire.*) Now just make yourself comfortable. (*Brings fender stool from fireplace.*) Put your feet up . . .

(*He does so.* JEAN *helps him.*)

. . . and I'll give orders you're not to be disturbed. (*Bends down and kisses him. She then starts to tiptoe across to window.*)
MAITLAND. If that sky pilot comes in again I'll wring his neck.
JEAN (*at window*). I'll see you're not disturbed, darling.

(*Exits quietly through French windows* L.)

(*After she has gone,* MAITLAND *sits up in chair and looks round. He must show his bewilderment in his face. After a few moments, he gets up and stands thinking. He goes to double doors* R., *listens for a second, looks round* L., *catches sight of telephone, looks at it—goes up to it, picks up receiver—*" Say, Exchange." *At that moment voices are heard in the garden. He sees a door half open down stage* L. *He goes through door* L. *and closes it behind him.*)

(*Enter through the windows,* JEAN, CHESTERMAN, LOUISE *and* AUBREY. JEAN *stops them at the entrance, signs to them to be quiet and walks softly over to chair. She cannot see* MAITLAND.)

Oh, dear, he's gone!

(AUBREY *comes down and looks under cushions and under settle.*)

AUBREY. I fear this is a very bad attack.

LOUISE (R.). We must find him.

CHESTERMAN (*with* LOUISE *a little up* C.). I'm afraid if he gets violent, he'll do someone an injury.

(AUBREY *sits on settle* L.)

JEAN. I should keep away if I were you, Mr. Brown. He swore he'd wring your neck just now.

AUBREY. That'll be nice.

JEAN. Oughtn't we to send for a doctor?

AUBREY. Why not a policeman. They are very firm on their feet.

JEAN. Oh, Mr. Brown, how can you say such things!

(*At this moment* HENERY *walks in through the windows from* L., *whistling.*)

CHESTERMAN. Hush! (*Remains up* L., *behind telephone table with* LOUISE.)

(AUBREY *sees him, puts his hand to his neck, starts to move nervously round the settle.* HENERY *watching him from* C. *begins to laugh, and imitates his walk, going towards him.* AUBREY *retreats.* HENERY *follows him round up stage* L. *end of settle.* AUBREY *makes a dash round settle, and finally runs to double doors* R.)

(*Exits* R.)

HENERY (*from back of settle*). He is a scream—that parson. (*Laughing.*)

LOUISE (*to* HENERY). How are you, Cousin George?

HENERY. Oh, I'm top-hole. (*Comes from behind settle in front to* JEAN R.C.) I've been looking for you.

JEAN (*soothingly*). Have you, dear? I've just been looking for you. Where have you been?

(JEAN R.—HENERY R.C.—LOUISE L.C.—CHESTERMAN *back of table* L.C.)

HENERY. Oh, just wandering round.

CHESTERMAN (*to* LOUISE). He remembers nothing about it. (*Goes to back of settle.*)

HENERY (*turns* L. *and sees* CHESTERMAN *looking suspiciously at him*). What are you looking at me like that for ? What's the matter with me ?

(JEAN *leads him to chair* R., *stroking his hand.*)

LOUISE (*to* CHESTERMAN). He's not quite right yet.

(CHESTERMAN *comes round settle to* C. LOUISE *drops down* L.)

JEAN (*to* HENERY). Nothing, dear, nothing.
HENERY. Well, don't do it. I don't like it.

(JEAN *takes one of his hands and starts stroking it. He snatches it away.*)

And leave my hands alone ! What are you messing me about for ?

(JEAN R. ; HENERY R.C. ; CHESTERMAN C. ; LOUISE L.)

JEAN. All right, darling. D'you know, if I were you I should sit down and rest a little bit.

CHESTERMAN. You're tired, I'm sure. (*Makes* HENERY *sit in chair* R.)

LOUISE. Worn out.
HENERY. I'm not tired, and I'm not worn out.
JEAN. No, no, of course you're not. All the same, sit down for a little. There, isn't that comfy ?
HENERY. Not very !
JEAN. Now, put your feet up. (*Puts his feet on stool.*)

(JEAN *signs to others, who go to windows quietly and stand watching.*)

Now I'll stay here quietly and you can go to sleep.
HENERY. What the deuce do I want to go to sleep for ?
JEAN. Well, there. (*Starts to massage his head gently.*)
HENERY. Leave my hair alone, can't you ? I think you've all gone mad.
JEAN. Wouldn't you like to tell me of some of your adventures ?
HENERY (*snappily*). No, I shouldn't ! I'm going to sleep. (*Pretends to sleep. Begins to snore softly.*)

(JEAN *kisses his head, and tiptoes across to others at the window, watching.*)

JEAN. He's all right now. He's gone off.

(HENERY *is wide awake and listening.* AUBREY *enters on tiptoe through double doors, steps over chair in front of grandfather clock, goes up to* JEAN *in window.*)

AUBREY. In case he shows fight I've got Giles standing by with a fork.

(HENERY *must express his feelings in his face.* LOUISE, AUBREY, CHESTERMAN *and* MISS EVERARD *all exeunt quietly, through French windows.*)

(HENERY *listens for a minute, then sits up. At that moment he sees the door down* L. *on the other side of the room open. He very cautiously gets up, and tiptoes across the room to the door. Arriving there, he stands with his ear against it in a listening attitude. Tries to look through hinge joint. Again it moves and he gradually begins to peer round the side.* MAITLAND *on the other side is hearing a noise, and he begins to look round, both heads coming round the corner of the door and meeting simultaneously. They glare at each other—hold picture and gradually* MAITLAND *comes out, step by step, and as he does so,* HENERY *recedes towards* C. *of stage. He falls over a chair* L.C. MAITLAND *grabs him, but* HENERY *throws him off.* MAITLAND *falls in the fireplace and* HENERY *escapes through French windows. He turns* L., *but sees* GILES *with a pitch-fork—he turns about and runs off* R. *into the garden.* GILES *is running after him just as* MAITLAND *is about to give chase.* GILES *holds* MAITLAND *at bay with the fork, thinking he is the same man.*)

MAITLAND. Not me, you fool! The other one! After him! (*Points* R. *of garden.*)

(GILES *runs off* R.)

It's a madhouse or a bunch of crooks! (*Furiously cross down* R.)

(*As he stands there,* CHESTERMAN, AUBREY, LOUISE *and* MISS MULLETT *creep in softly through window from* L.)

JEAN (*to others*). He's awake! (*Approaches* MAITLAND *quietly.*) George!

(MAITLAND *wheels round savagely.*)

MAITLAND. Who's the man who's just gone out?
JEAN. Man, darling?
ALL. What man?
MAITLAND. Like me, he's gone out of that window—after him!
ALL. The impostor! After him!

(*Exeunt* CHESTERMAN, JEAN, MISS MULLETT *and* MAITLAND *through windows to garden* R.)

(LOUISE *and* AUBREY *regard each other helplessly.*)

AUBREY. Louise, there are two of them! (*Comes down and falls into chair* R.)
LOUISE. And twenty-five of yours in cash! (*In chair* L.C.)

AUBREY. What!!! Have I lent it to the wrong one ?
LOUISE. Of course you have.
AUBREY. Oh, love a duck!
LOUISE. Aubrey—I've got an idea.
AUBREY (*gets out of chair and shrinks away to the fireplace*). I'll never die again as long as I live.
LOUISE. No, darling, you shan't. (*Springs to her feet.*) This time you shall come to life.
AUBREY. Oh, what's the good of that ?
LOUISE (R.C.). What's the good of it ? Listen. Clear out and put on an old suit of clothes—make yourself as dirty and untidy as possible.
AUBREY. Yes ? (*Advancing, interested.*)
LOUISE. Wait till they're all in here and then stagger in through the garden—in a dazed condition.
AUBREY. And get promptly arrested for fraud.
LOUISE. Don't be so absurd ! Act !! You've lost your memory. The shock of the explosion ! You weren't killed. You've been wandering about ever since.
AUBREY. By Jove ! (*Crosses* LOUISE *and goes up* C.—*turns.*).
LOUISE (*facing* AUBREY). You've come back here—you see me —the old home—it all comes back to you—they don't contradict you and—(*triumphantly*)—the money's ours !

(*Voices heard off.*)

AUBREY. Right ! I'll do it !
LOUISE. Quick ! I hear them. (R.C.)

(AUBREY *bolts out through double doors* R.)

(*At the moment*, MAITLAND, JEAN, CHESTERMAN *and* MISS MULLETT *come in through the windows from* L. *excitedly.*)

MAITLAND. He's got clean away ! (*Down* L.)
CHESTERMAN. I suppose you *are* really George Maitland ? (*Behind table* L.C.)
MAITLAND. Say, has this house gone plumb crazy ?

(MISS MULLETT *to* R. ; LOUISE R.C. ; MAITLAND L. ; JEAN C. ; CHESTERMAN *behind telephone table.*)

LOUISE. Certainly not, Cousin George, but——
MAITLAND (*comes* C.). Well, if this house is the English idea of hospitality to a man who's come three thousand miles, it's me for Mexico every time.

JEAN. But, George dear——

MAITLAND. You keep out of the way, Jean! I'm not blaming you. Now, Mr. Lawyer, let's hear from you.

CHESTERMAN. You see, Mr. Maitland, we've had two impostors here in the last two days.

MAITLAND. Well, that's not my funeral.

MISS MULLETT (*sitting* R.; *to* LOUISE). Whose funeral's he talking about, dear? Is someone else dead now?

LOUISE. No, auntie, no one is dead.

MISS MULLETT. Then why is he talking about funerals?

CHESTERMAN. No doubt you've got papers in your pocket to prove your identity, Mr. Maitland?

MAITLAND. Papers! I'm as full of papers as a bookstall. And if I could have got someone to talk horse sense when I first arrived you'd have got 'em long ago.

JEAN. Louise, where's Mr. Brown?

(MAITLAND *top of table* L.C.; CHESTERMAN, *behind settle.*)

LOUISE (*nervously*). Er—I don't know.

CHESTERMAN. Oh, doubtless he'll turn up again in a minute.

LOUISE. Yes, I shouldn't be a bit surprised if he does.

MAITLAND (*giving papers to* CHESTERMAN). Just take a look over those, Mr. Lawyer. If anyone wants to dispute my identity, come on, let's start disputing.

(JEAN *leads* MAITLAND *to front of settle. They sit.*)

CHESTERMAN (*examining papers* L.C.). Well, it's something to know we've found the rightful heir at last, Mr. Maitland. It looks as if all our troubles were over now.

MISS MULLETT. What's all the trouble about, my dear?

LOUISE. There's no trouble at all, auntie. This is really Mr. George Maitland.

MISS MULLETT. They've all said that, my dear. You're sure to find he isn't.

JEAN. George—you can kiss me.

(*They kiss.* LOUISE *goes down* R.; MISS MULLETT R. *in her chair;* CHESTERMAN *reading papers comes down* L; JEAN *and* MAITLAND *on settle.*)

I could have told you anywhere, George, by the way you kiss!

MISS MULLETT. That's the third man she's kissed in two days.

(AUBREY *appears on the terrace from* R.: *he wanders past one window and stops at the other, gazes into the room, and staggers in looking about very dazed; he is very dirty, and is wearing clothes all odd, a light coat, dark trousers, an old straw hat and white canvas shoes; he carries a banjo, looking like a very low-down minstrel.*)

LOUISE (*with a shriek, comes* C.). Aubrey—my husband—alive! Alive! You're not a ghost?

(AUBREY *twangs banjo. Hold*—PICTURE.)

(MISS MULLETT R. *standing front of her chair;* LOUISE R.C.; AUBREY C.; JEAN *and* MAITLAND, *having risen, stand front of settle;* CHESTERMAN L. *All lean forward facing* AUBREY.)

AUBREY (*pretending to be dazed*). Who are you?
LOUISE. I'm Louise—Aubrey—your own little wife.
AUBREY. Where am I? (*Puts banjo down against chair* L.C.)
LOUISE. In your home, darling—your old home.
AUBREY. My old home! The same old home—the same little wife!
LOUISE. And here is auntie. . . . (*Indicating* MISS MULLETT.)
AUBREY. The same old auntie! The same old knitting!
LOUISE. And there's Mr. Chesterman, the lawyer . . .
AUBREY. The same old liar!
LOUISE (*indicating* CHESTERMAN). . . . who came to tell us about the money.
AUBREY. Money? Money? I've heard of that somewhere.
LOUISE. Aubrey, can't you remember? The blasted powder! The explosion!
AUBREY. Explosion! Explosion! (*Suddenly changing his voice.*) Oh, it all comes back to me! (*Throws his hat off.*)
ALL. Yes, yes!
AUBREY. Like—like a returned cheque.
ALL. Yes, yes!
AUBREY. I was alone—by myself—in the shed.
JEAN. Yes, yes!
AUBREY. I was working.
ALL. Yes, yes!
AUBREY. I don't know why.
ALL. No, no!
AUBREY. Suddenly there was a crash!
ALL. Yes, yes!
AUBREY. A fleet of shame——
LOUISE. A shame of fleet. (*Trying to help him.*)
AUBREY. A sheem of flate.
ALL. Yes, yes!
AUBREY. And—and—and everything seemed to go up, up, up, then it came down, down, down, and round and round and round, and here we are again!

(AUBREY *and* LOUISE *embrace.*)

(*Telephone bell.*)

CHESTERMAN. I'll answer the 'phone, Mr. Allington.

(*Going up behind settle,* CHESTERMAN *takes receiver, holding imaginary conversation.*)

MAITLAND. Yes, but where do I come in ? (*Advances* L.C. *to* AUBREY, JEAN *behind him.*)

AUBREY (R.C.). You don't !

LOUISE. Aubrey dear, this is Cousin George from Mexico.

AUBREY. So you're the fellow who gets the money when I'm dead.

MAITLAND (*angrily*). But you are dead.

AUBREY. Oh no, I'm not !

MAITLAND. Well, there's something crooked about the whole business I want explained. Here am I fetched all the way from Vera Cruz. . . .

AUBREY (*to* MAITLAND). Don't mention that woman's name ! I'm alive and the money's mine.

MAITLAND. The money's mine, you're dead.

AUBREY. You can dispute it until you're blue in the face.

MAITLAND. The money's mine, and I'm going to have it.

AUBREY. If you can get it, you're welcome to it.

(CHESTERMAN *leaves 'phone, comes* C. *between* AUBREY *and* MAITLAND, MAITLAND *and* JEAN L.C.; CHESTERMAN C.; LOUISE *and* AUBREY R.C.; MISS MULLETT R.)

CHESTERMAN (*loudly*). One moment, please, one moment ! Gentlemen ! I've just received a message from my office. Your brother's estate has just been cleared up and I am now in a position to pay over a cheque for the whole amount.

MAITLAND. You pay that money to me. (*Brightly.*)

AUBREY. You'll do nothing of the kind ; you'll pay that money to me.

CHESTERMAN. One moment, please. After deducting expenses, death duties and the usual fees, the estate has realized £87,600.

MAITLAND. You pay that to me.

AUBREY. No, to me. (*Very brightly.*)

CHESTERMAN. Gentlemen, I said eighty-seven thousand six hundred less a confiscation of certain money by the Mexican Government, leaving the sum total of one pound four shillings and fourpence-halfpenny.

(AUBREY *with a look of despair staggers towards the settle.*)

LOUISE. Aubrey !

AUBREY. Yes, darling ?

LOUISE. I've got an idea!

(AUBREY *dives under the settle.*)

                JEAN AND MAITLAND   AUBREY
                       L.C.   *under settle.*
                CHESTERMAN
                       C.

    LOUISE
      R.C.

MISS MULLETT
  R

CURTAIN.

FURNITURE PLOT

ACTS I, II, III

Long fender-stool, at fire.
Small Jacobean writing-table, set L.C.
Queen Anne high-backed chair, set extreme R.
Jacobean arm-chair, set R. (for MISS MULLETT).
Three small Jacobean chairs, set at opening of Act I—one up stage by bookcase, one R. of table R.C., and one at top of same table.
Grandfather clock (in going order).
Jacobean sideboard, set R. of R. double doors.
Jacobean settle, set L.C. at angle facing R.
Gate-legged table (4′ 6″ × 3′ 6″), set R.C.
Carpet and rugs.
Curb fender.
Small Jacobean footstool, set L. of MISS MULLETT's chair (Acts II and III).
Bookcase.
Pedestal with flowers in bowl, set L.C. up stage.
Low Jacobean arm-chair, set extreme L.
Figure holding electrolier, set extreme L. wall.
Jacobean cabinet with drawer, set R. of window recess.

PROPERTY PLOT

ACT I

PROPERTIES ON STAGE

Photograph album, set in drawer of sideboard R.
Speaking-tube, set on R. wall of window recess above cabinet.
Electric bell-push, set fireplace R. down stage.
Books for bookcase.
Ash tray, set on table L.C.
Telephone, set on table L.C.
Cigarette box, with cigarettes, set table L.C.
Cigarette box, set on sideboard.
Breakfast service for two, set on table R.C.
White cloth, set on table R.C.
Rose bowl, set on table R.C.
Letters and writs, set on table R.C.
Times newspaper, set on back of chair R. of table R.C.
Pewter pot containing flowers, set on sideboard R.
Large candlesticks and bowl on fire shelf.
Electric sconces on walls.
Horns, crossbow and large plaque on walls.
Crimson ramblers on balustrade.
Hollyhocks behind balustrade.

PROPERTIES OFF L.

Gardener's basket.
Property cucumber.
Three china eggs.
Watering-can.
Property bricks.
Maroon in a metal drum with wire cover for explosion.
Smoke candle.
Thunder sheet.
Telephone bell in prompt corner.

PROPERTIES OFF R.

Butler's tray containing coffee-pot (coffee), cream-jug (milk).
Entrée dish containing sponge cakes.
Toast in rack.
Three breakfast plates.
Bunch of flowers for GILES.
Will form for CHESTERMAN and attaché-case.
Knitting for MISS MULLETT.
Spectacles for MISS MULLETT.
Telegram on salver.

ACT II

PROPERTIES SET ON STAGE

Tatler newspaper on settle.
Afternoon tea cloth in sideboard cupboard.

PROPERTIES SET OFF L.

Gardener's basket with property gooseberries.

PROPERTIES OFF R.

Salver with teapot (containing tea) and empty muffin-dish.
Tea-tray.
Cake-stand with cakes.
Cream-jug.
Sugar bowl.
Afternoon teacups and saucers, spoons, etc.
Suit of clothes.
Shirt for LOUISE.
Boat cushions and carpet, rudder and lines for AUBREY.
Salver for SPRULES.
Glass of water.

ACT III

PROPERTIES SET ON STAGE

Cigarette box on sideboard R.

PROPERTIES OFF L.

Banjo for AUBREY.
Hayfork for GILES.
Legal documents for MAITLAND.
Matches in box for CHESTERMAN.
Bank-notes.
Cigarette case with cigarettes for AUBREY, and horn-rimmed spectacles.

LIGHTING PLOT

AMBERS R. AND L. PERCHES

ACT I. OPEN.
    Battens and floats full up, amber and white.
    1 small length amber and white—doorway L.
    1 length amber and white between French windows, L.C.
    1 length amber and white ground row behind balustrade, L.C.
    1 length amber and white over doorway, R.
    2 ½-Watt flood lamps on back cloth white frost.
    1 ½-Watt flood lamp, 2 amber mediums without frost behind window, R.C.
        At Cue, check down back lighting.

ACTS II AND III.
    Same as Act I, except that the 2 ½-Watt flood or arcs on back cloth change to amber.

PRINTED IN GREAT BRITAIN BY
THE LONGDUNN PRESS LTD BRISTOL
MADE IN ENGLAND

www.ingramcontent.com/pod-product-compliance
Ingram Content Group UK Ltd.
Pitfield, Milton Keynes, MK11 3LW, UK
UKHW021840210426
5322IPUK00022B/387